Parenting Through PLAY

Parenting Through PLAY

Creative Strategies for Building Better Behavior, Deeper Connection, and Positive Communication

Dr. Kim Van Dusen

Countryman Press

An Imprint of W. W. Norton & Company
Independent Publishers Since 1923

For information about permission to reproduce selections from this book, write to
Permissions, Countryman Press, 500 Fifth Avenue, New York, NY 10110

For information about special discounts for bulk purchases, please contact
W. W. Norton Special Sales at specialsales@wwnorton.com or 800-233-4830

Manufacturing by Lakeside Book Company
Production manager: Devon Zahn

Countryman Press
www.countrymanpress.com

An imprint of W. W. Norton & Company, Inc.
500 Fifth Avenue, New York, NY 10110
www.wwnorton.com

Authorized EU representative: EAS, Mustamäe tee 50, 10621 Tallinn, Estonia

978-1-68268-973-8

10 9 8 7 6 5 4 3 2 1

To my children—you are my entire world.
I love you both with my whole heart.

Contents

Preface

Hi! I'm Dr. Kim. It's so nice to meet you. I am a mom of two and a doctoral-level licensed marriage and family therapist. I'm also a nationally recognized registered play therapist specializing in children, both neurotypical and neurodiverse, in the toddler to elementary (ages two through ten) group, the ultimate audience for this book. For nearly twenty years I've helped parents connect playfully with their children to solve everyday behavioral problems and find their way to positive behaviors through a solution-focused lens. And for almost a decade, I've also taught hundreds of graduate-level therapy students about the essence of play as well as the dynamics of the parent-child relationship. For years I led a program to formally implement a positive behavioral support system in more than twenty elementary schools, and every day I interact with a large online audience of parents looking for help in navigating their children's undesirable behaviors. I also conduct therapeutic play sessions with my private practice families. This book is not only for parents; it's also for therapists, teachers, coaches, pediatricians, grandparents, and any other adult caregiver looking to connect positively, peacefully, and playfully with children.

Parenting can be both rewarding and challenging, especially when faced with behaviors or emotional reactivity that may seem difficult to navigate. Positive, solution-focused approaches paired with play therapy techniques offer a dynamic framework to empower parents and foster connection and growth within families. These methods emphasize strengths, solutions, and the power of play as a means of communication, connection, and healing.

When a child asks their parent to play with them, they are communicating, "I need to be connected with you and want to be loved by you" and "Play makes me feel safe when I am having a positive interaction with you."

Solution-focused strategies encourage parents to shift from problem-centered thinking to identifying and building on what is already working. Positive behavior interventions help parents learn to set attainable goals, celebrate small wins, and reinforce positive behaviors, creating a sense of progress and hope. Play therapy complements these approaches by offering children a safe nonverbal outlet for expressing emotions, resolving conflicts, and building coping skills. Through child-led play, parents gain insights into their child's world, enabling more effective communication and deeper understanding. Interventions such as role-play, therapeutic storytelling, and play-based parenting activities equip families with tools to address challenges collaboratively. Positive discipline techniques, combined with reflective listening, help parents model empathy and guide their children toward healthy emotional regulation.

Not only does play serve as a mechanism for children to regulate emotions, it also affects how they behave and how they perceive and navigate life. Playing is how children make sense of their world and learn how to understand it. Ultimately, these approaches empower parents to nurture their child's unique potential while fostering a supportive and playful family environment. By integrating positive, solution-focused play therapy techniques, parents can cultivate resilience, strengthen relationships, and create an emotionally safe home where children and parents alike can thrive.

Introduction

> "All of our dreams can come true, if we have the courage to
> pursue them."
>
> —Walt Disney

I felt my cheeks get hot and flushed as my son deliberately refused to listen to me and follow my directions. I had asked him to leave while he was playing and he vetoed me. I got it—he was playing with some friends after school, which is what therapists call a preferred activity, and he didn't want to leave—but it was time to go. Asking wasn't working. Telling wasn't working. I felt the eyes of the other parents on me, waiting to see how the parenting expert would handle this. Weren't my children supposed to be perfectly well behaved and role models for other children?

Feeling judged and desperate, this professional play therapist bribed her son with a treat if we left. When even that didn't work, I went to punishment and threatened to take away video games if he didn't comply. When that didn't work either, I started to panic. I tried to gently pick him up, but he said no and squirmed out of my reach.

For goodness' sake, didn't I specialize in helping children experiencing emotional and behavioral challenges? Didn't I give advice almost every day about how parents could help their children behave? So why wasn't my own child behaving in this moment? The power struggle was real, and it was getting ugly. I was reaching a breaking point and knew I had to think quickly. I took a deep, calming breath and had a moment of clarity. I needed to follow my own advice. The standard parenting responses clearly weren't working, so I needed to think creatively. I needed to think outside the box. So I put on my play therapist hat and decided to try using a preferred play activity to lure my son away from his friends. I didn't need bribes or punishments. I just needed to engage with him in a playful way.

"Choo choo!" I yelled. "The train is leaving in one minute!"

My son turned around almost immediately and said, "I want to go on the train, Mommy!"

I smiled and exhaled for the first time in ten minutes. I walked over to our car and hopped in. I started the ignition and put the window down and yelled again, "All aboard! The train is leaving now!"

He turned and said goodbye to his friends and got in the car with no hesitation. The other parents looked at me a little dumbfounded. As we drove away, he leaned out the window and waved goodbye to his friends. Then he turned to me and said, "Mommy, can you have the train pick me up every day after school?" Of course I said yes, and that's what I did. We never again had a problem leaving when I said it was time to go.

You'd think I had performed a magic trick. What I really did was speak my child's language.

I often get asked what the secret is to get children to behave. It takes nurturing and patience, as all parenting does, but also a secret ingredient that doesn't come naturally to a lot of parents: play. *Play is the essence of parenting.*

When a new client tells me during our intake conversation that their child is misbehaving and nothing is working to change their behavior, one of the first questions I ask is how often they're spending time with their child in a playful way. More often than not, they describe days filled with caring for their child, appointments, work, errands, and other necessary responsibilities where play isn't part of the equation. Even parents who care for their children full-time are often so busy they don't spend much dedicated, undistracted time with their children. But almost every time we shift the *parent's* behavior to include even a little bit of playtime with their child, the child's negative behaviors diminish, the parent-child bond deepens, the parent is less stressed, and there is more positivity and peacefulness in the home.

Believe it or not, you can change almost any problematic behavior using child-friendly, play-based tools, and it doesn't require loads of time. Parenting through play is the best-kept secret in town. If it's used properly to engage with your child, so many parenting struggles very quickly turn into parenting wins.

Play-based techniques and interventions are well researched and highly effective, but at present they remain an underutilized behavioral modification modality. Most parenting books do not focus on play-based strategies to modify behavior, and the few that mention therapeutic play or play-based parenting don't go into sufficient depth. Years ago, I recognized this void in the parenting space, so I decided to create a new, unique parenting style, with methods and strategies grounded in an approach that is play-based, solution-focused, and designed to elicit positive behaviors rather than punish children for negative or undesirable ones. Play, solutions, and positive reinforcement are the trifecta of how to get children to behave. These evidence-based methods work because they connect with children in a manner they intuitively understand—the universal language of play.

This book is uniquely dedicated to this powerful and compassionate approach, and it presents the concepts in a modern, relatable, and practical way. Play-based parenting is an innovative and revolutionary overarching approach to child-rearing and an everyday way to parent more effectively. This book is designed to get fast-acting solutions into the hands of parents who need them quickly, and to help guide and support families through their parenting journey, using play in their favor and to its fullest potential. You may be unsure if you have what it takes to be a play-based parent, or what I like to call a "Play-It-Out" parent, but let me assure you, you do! I've helped even the busiest and most play-reluctant parents rediscover their inner child and sense of fun, and I'll show you how you can do that, too. With just the willingness to try something new, something that will benefit both you and your child, parenting can feel much more manageable and, honestly, a lot more enjoyable.

Each chapter will be concise and straight to the point for parents needing a quick yet effective way to help their children in the moment of a problematic behavior. Instead of being filled with theoretical, scientific, and hard-to-understand concepts that do not seem practical or applicable to specific everyday parenting moments, this book provides straightforward "how-to" prompts as well as step-by-step tips and instructions on how to handle a variety of behavioral situations. I write with a careful balance of professional, expert-level parenting advice for the everyday parent with a sprinkle of heartfelt, personal, and relatable stories from my own motherhood experience.

All parents need tools, and this book will provide a plethora of evidence-based resources and fun, proactive solutions every parent can add to their toolbox. It will help parents feel that they are not alone and provide support when it's needed most. It will help families spend less time struggling with disruptive behaviors and more time enjoying each other's company. Welcome. I'm glad you're here.

PART I

The Fundamentals of Parenting Through Play

Chapter 1

The Essence of Play-It-Out Parenting

> "Toys are a child's words and play is the child's language."
> —Garry Landreth

DO YOUR CHILDREN STRUGGLE WITH TANTRUM BEHAVIORS when they don't get their way or obtain something they want? Are they masters at finding loopholes between caregivers and using you against each other? Do your children have a meltdown when you ask them to stop a preferred activity and transition to something else? Or perhaps they completely defy you when you ask them to clean up their toys or their room. Maybe your child flat-out refuses to eat what you made for dinner. Or possibly it's bath time or bedtime or getting your children up in the morning and out the door in time for school that devolves into a power struggle.

What if I told you that you could minimize or even eliminate your child's challenging behaviors with a few moderately quick and easy changes? Want to get rid of power struggles and standoffs? No problem. Want to lessen tantrums and meltdowns? That's doable! Want your child to do their chores or homework without defiance or complaint? I can make that happen. Better yet, you can make that happen!

As a mom of two young children, I know all too well how much we invest into our relationship with our children and how much we sacrifice for their well-being. We do everything we can to protect them, nurture them, and provide environments where they'll thrive. If you're like many of today's parents (the word *parent* is used in this book to represent the wide range of adult caregivers who raise children), you begin preparing yourself well before your bundle of joy even arrives, spending hours online researching the latest parenting trends and recommendations, and reading multiple books written by parenting experts.

But inevitably, no matter how prepared you feel, there comes a time when you hit a snag—your baby becomes a willful toddler who melts down in stores or a school-age child who struggles with listening, following directions, and being respectful—and none of the recommended advice seems to help. You then realize your child is unique and doesn't fit into a cookie-cutter mold. So where does this leave you?

In need of quick and effective solutions, you watch a bazillion social media videos and read a plethora of blog posts on how to get your child to behave, but you end up inundated with information. Or you may try one parenting style after another, method by method, and when those don't help, you start to feel like you're failing. Meanwhile your child's behavior curveballs keep coming and your patience dwindles. You start questioning everything you've ever known as a parent, and you suddenly feel isolated, like you're stranded all alone on a deserted island. You're doing the best you can, but it just doesn't seem to be good enough, leaving you drained and desperate for support. What you need are new and fresh ideas—something quick and practical, not complicated and theoretical. Something you and your child can both benefit from.

That's where I come in. Between my own children, my clients, the student therapists I teach, and the online community of parents who reach out to me for help, I have heard and seen it all. Believe me, I know what it's like when your child misbehaves and no longer seems to respect anything you say or do. But I also know what it's like when a glimmer of light breaks through and you find a new method of parenting that not only works to solve your child's problematic behaviors but actually makes parenting more fun. For me that glimmer of light is positive play-based behavioral interventions, and in this book I'm going to show you how it can be the same for you in your parenting journey. I'll guide you through everything you need to know about play-based Play-It-Out parenting and provide you with new, unique, practical, and effective ways to help you parent your children and encourage their best behavior. These concepts will transform your child's behavior while changing the dynamics of your home and your relationship with your child.

Why Children Respond to Play

Most parents don't think of playing when their child is acting out. In fact, most parents think the exact opposite and respond in punitive ways. This is perfectly understandable, as most of the models we've been exposed to recommend "extinguishing" unwanted behaviors by ignoring them (for example, not responding to whining) or discouraging those behaviors by punishment (taking away a privilege or desired object) or isolation (putting a child on time-out or sending them to their room). And let's face it, it can feel deeply counterintuitive to respond to a child's problematic behavior with anything involving play because it seems like we're rewarding bad behavior. Or maybe play becomes the reward, not the necessity, when a parent says, "Stop playing around and get back to work" or allows a child to go play after their work is done. Let me assure you, if you want your child to behave and you'd like to have a more peaceful home, play has to be a priority in the way you parent. To do this, you simply need to communicate with your child on their level—and yes, that might include getting down on the floor with them—and use "words" they understand: toys, games, puzzles, or any material they can play with, such as clay or kinetic sand. The options are endless, and we'll explore many throughout the book. For now, let's look at a little of the theory behind why play-based methods work.

Children respond to play because it is their universal language. As Rogers and Sawyers (1988) said in their book, *Play in the Lives of Children*, "play is life for young children." A parent must be able to speak and understand a child's language to communicate with them in a meaningful way, much less affect their behavior. Even very young children will respond better when you respect and interact with their world in a relatable way. Think for a moment about how children connect with each other. They play. This differs from how adults connect because adults don't play, they talk. And parents often forget this when they are parenting their children. A parent's attitude toward play matters and also makes a difference in how children play. If a parent doesn't value play and dismisses it, there will be a disconnect between the parent and the child that leads to behavioral conflict. Vandenberg (1985) contended that parents should value play because "it's the main feature of what it means to be human."

For example, let's say a child misplaces a beloved stuffed animal, so they instinctively scribble lost and found posters and start taping them on the walls around the house. The child is using play to problem-solve and ask for help from other family members to find the misplaced toy. Are you the parent who embraces the playful effort to communicate and help your child start a rescue mission to find the stuffed animal, or do you get upset that your child put scribbly pieces of paper around your house and now it's messy and you're anxious about who will clean it up? That parent may say, "Just use your words and ask us to help you find your toy" instead of trying to see the situation and efforts through the child's eyes to solve their problem in a creative way. The fact is, children don't think like parents, and parents often forget how to think like a child, so our interactions with our children begin with a significant language barrier. This is why children don't always respond positively to talking with an adult, even their own parent. Most young children don't yet have the language skills to talk with or listen to adults, especially when the adults are speaking in abstractions or when the child is in a state of emotional dysregulation. In fact, when a child is dysregulated, stressed, or overstimulated, we can't expect them to respond well to a typical parenting technique that requires emotional regulation as well as critical-thinking and language skills they don't have. This is why trying to reason with upset children or jumping immediately to a punishment leads to even more defiance or disengagement.

There is another way, one that eliminates the language barrier between children and adults. The language of play is intuitively understood by children, including those who are upset, who have speech and language delays or selective mutism, and even many nonverbal children with an autism diagnosis. Indeed, these instances are where play-based interventions can be most valuable. But across the board, play is a parent's best tool for communicating and connecting with their child. Recent research has shown that up to 80 percent of children experience positive mental, emotional, social, and behavioral benefits from play-based therapeutic interventions (Bratton et al. 2005; Bratton et al. 2013).

Playing with a child builds trust and safety, and it's one of the most effective ways to create a significant attachment between parent and child. You'll need to establish that sense of deep connection and trust before trying to shift a child's behavior in a positive direction. Play-based methods also work best when they're used regularly, as part of an overall parenting approach, rather than as a last-ditch intervention. Once this shift in parenting takes place, using play to parent becomes less foreign, and children more easily adapt and adjust their behavior in more positive ways. And within the more peaceful environment that play-based parenting fosters, where a child feels safe and deeply connected to their parent, many unwanted behaviors simply don't come up like they once did.

We also know that for children, play is an essential component for learning and healthy development. Research has shown that young children learn best through meaningful play experiences, which activate calming mechanisms that make it easier to acquire and retain information. Through play, children learn to build language skills and communicate with others, express and regulate their emotions, develop critical problem-solving skills, and yes, modify their behavior. According to Caldwell (1985), "The most important foundation for children's healthy development is the reciprocally pleasurable play between adults and children; playful play is related to all things that we want young children to learn to do."

These concepts are also emphasized by Rogers and Sawyers, who argue that "on the surface children's play looks deceptively simple," which is why I believe it is dismissed and undermined when it comes to parenting and behavior modification. But for children, play is serious business! And it can be a parent's best friend.

The Play-Based Parent

Play-based parenting comes more easily to some than to others, but let me assure you that everyone can get the hang of it if they are open to it. The methods and techniques are simple and quick—and yes, they are fun! It just takes a willingness to try something different.

When I teach a play therapy class, speak at a conference, host a parenting seminar, or even see a family in private practice, I have a secret weapon that helps unlock parents' psyches so they can start shifting their adult-minded perspective into a childlike one. It's a particular play exercise that helps them let go of their inhibitions in order to get in touch with their inner child. I challenge them to a snowball fight.

Yep, you read that right. Without much warning or explanation,

I bring out a set of soft cotton snowballs and start throwing them around. And then I ask them to join in. It's fascinating to see the transformation that takes place when you ask parents to play. At first some parents are quite timid and will even sit with their hands crossed across their chest, waiting for this dreaded exercise to be over. But after a few minutes, a change transpires. Parents start smiling or even chuckling, and you can see their jaw and shoulders loosen. Childlike competition starts to emerge, and soon enough the parents are in a full-fledged snowball fight, tossing every ball that comes near them across the room, ducking at balls thrown in their direction, and laughing straight from the belly. They aren't worried about what anyone else thinks of them in that moment. They are fully present and fully engaged.

This is the feeling I teach to parents who have lost that playfulness with their children. It's a freeing feeling that eliminates the anxiety caused by day-to-day stressors of adulting after we have children. As parents, we focus on keeping our children safe, ferrying them to various places, budgeting and planning for their future, cleaning (and cleaning again), and handling the inevitable moments of marital discord that arise from time to time. We often forget how to let go and release the stress associated with those daily responsibilities. There should be a both/and perspective here, but we often lean toward either/or, and play gets sacrificed for the work of parenting. So how can we reclaim a sense of play when we can't wage a spontaneous snowball fight?

All you need to do is cultivate a purposeful play pocket of time! How about a spontaneous dance party? When there is tension and anxiety flowing throughout the home—when the parent and child are dysregulated, overwhelmed, or overstimulated, resulting in yelling, crying, meltdowns, defiance, and punishments—I often suggest that my clients turn on some music and get moving. The physical movement regulates the nervous system and releases stress and more often than not sparks some much-needed laughter that cuts right through the tension.

Not the dancing type? Go on a walk to get your body moving and get some fresh air flowing through your lungs. While you are outside, go on a scavenger hunt with your child and have them find things like leaves, sticks, and rocks that they can collect while you sip tea, water, coffee, or an energy drink. This breaks up the monotony of the day yet requires little to no direct parenting. By the time you get back, you will both feel refreshed and even forget you were upset or stressed in the first place. It's an excellent way to pause, play, and reset, giving you the ability to get through the rest of the day.

If it's a warm day, I recommend running through the sprinklers or playing in a sandbox. Yes, that's right. Get on your bathing suit and feel the water on your skin. Let go! I promise, the combination of the sensory experience plus the play will lower your cortisol (the stress hormone) levels and help you thrive for the remainder of the day. If that doesn't sound like fun, have your child play in the dirt or sand while you practice a grounding exercise by walking barefoot on the grass or moving your toes through the sand. It will be a similar sensory experience that will lower your cortisol, restore your energy, and be an effective reset for both you and your child.

There is a play experience that will appeal to every parent. I've found that when parents have inhibitions or anxiety around play, most of the time it actually comes down to a parent who is simply exhausted and doesn't have the patience or energy to play with their child. We've all been there. Your child asks you to play with them after a long, busy day, and you just don't have the energy. Playing is the very last thing you want to do! What you really want is to have a few moments to yourself or just lie down and sleep.

What happens next? Often, it's one of three scenarios: You muster the last of your energy and (reluctantly) play with your child, you reject and refuse, or, on really bad days, you lose your cool. Clearly, none of these outcomes are optimal for you or your child. When you refuse or lose your temper, your child feels rejected and distraught, you feel guilty, and usually you give in, only to feel more resentful. Even when you do manage to get in a little playtime, your engagement is likely half-hearted and can easily result in the same outcome: more guilt and resentment. But there are plenty of ways you can play with your child that don't take much energy, gobs of time, or loads of creativity and imagination. Our children have energy, creativity, and imagination in abundance, so on days when you have nothing left in the tank, you can leave all that to them. What they most want is our presence, and you can be present as a passive play-based parent even on your most exhausted days.

A Play-Based Mindset

To get a notion of your readiness to engage in play-based parenting, let's see where you are with having a play-based mindset. The exercise that follows will help determine what you might need to do to shift your perspective before many of the interventions in this book will work. It will also help you see that there are ways you can handle a situation differently, including play-based responses you never thought of, to help your child behave in a more positive way.

Which answer in the table on the next page most accurately describes your response?

As you've no doubt gathered, the responses in the right-hand column are all play-based interventions. Did you know it was even possible to turn cleaning into a game—one that inspires the behavior and the results you've been hoping for? Did you know that with a simple, economical toy like a sand timer, you can signal to your child that their feelings matter while teaching them that they're capable of regulating their own emotions? These are classic examples of how play-based parenting offers effective solutions in the midst of difficult moments.

Being a play-based parent takes imagination, creativity, spontaneity, flexibility, and childlike thinking. If you feel like you're fresh

When my child has a tantrum, I . . .	Send them to their room	Try to talk to them about it	Actively ignore them	Start playing and wait for them to regulate and join
When my child doesn't clean up their toys/room after being told three times, I . . .	Discipline them	Take something away	Try to bribe them	Turn cleaning into a game
When my child is pouting, I . . .	Tell them to stop	Ignore them	Punish them	Get a sand timer and give them time to process their mood
When my child has trouble getting ready for school on time, I . . .	Get upset	Tell them to hurry up	Leave without them	Play a game like "The Floor Is Lava" to get them out the door quickly

out of all these qualities, just hang on. Let me show you how easy it can be. A play-based parenting style can be adopted with a mindset shift.

Let's start with the basics. In addition to putting a higher value on play, here are the fundamentals of having a play-based parenting perspective.

Spontaneity and Flexibility: First and foremost, you need the spontaneity to try something new in the moment and an open mindset to try something different. Sometimes in session when I suggest a parent try something foreign to them, they shut it down and insist it won't work, even when they haven't tried it yet or have only tried it once. Even if you're at the point where you feel like you've tried everything and nothing works, the fact that you're reading this book tells me you're willing to give it another shot. No matter where you are in your parenting journey, having an open mind and some spontaneity will allow you to try a new parenting method. For the concepts in this book to be executed properly, you have to be willing to try them wholeheartedly.

Imagination and Creativity: To be a successful play-based parent, you need to release your inhibitions and connect with your childlike self. You need to be playful and willing to think outside the box when coming up with ways to connect with your child and manage their behavior. We are trained to think and act a certain way as a parent, as if it's a math equation: child misbehaves + frustrated parent = parent yelling and child being disciplined. But that isn't the most effective way to help a child transform their behavior. Instead of using the standard repertoire of time-outs, bribes, or taking possessions away when a child misbehaves, play-based parenting invites you to think creatively, using a playful, childlike imagination.

A Regulated Self: Before you can be an effective play-based parent, you need to be in a regulated state of mind. Trust me, I know what it's like to be stressed, overwhelmed, and flustered as a parent. Parenting is hard work! Even now, after all my training and practice, when I am not regulated I often revert back to old parenting ways, raising my voice at my children and telling them to go to their rooms when they do something wrong. Because I am dysregulated or overstimulated, my mind is closed off to thinking in a play-based way. But if I am regulated and calm, my mind is open to thinking up all sorts of playful ideas that might solve the problem at hand. Whether I need a few minutes of silence in my room, some fresh air outside, or a brisk walk to get my body moving, I need to regulate myself before parenting a difficult situation for the best outcome, not only for me as the parent but also for my child.

So next time your child misbehaves, follow these steps:

1. Ask yourself, am I calm? If not, take a moment to regulate yourself and get your mind in the right headspace.
2. Acknowledge your child's emotion and address the behavior. Show empathy, listen, and validate. Let them feel seen and heard.
3. Ask yourself, what is a play-based way to handle this situation? Before jumping to anger or a consequence, try to redirect your child's current energy in a more positive way by using one of the interventions in this book.

Here's what it can look like. For years, I struggled to get my children to clean up the stairs. I tried everything: writing notes and taping them on the stairway, putting the misplaced items in little baskets with their name on them in the middle of the stairs, bribing them, and even disciplining them when they walked over the mess on the stairs for the thousandth time. You name it, I tried it.

But I finally put on my play-based parenting hat and came up with a unique solution. I had my children stand at the bottom of the stairs while I stood at the top, where they would throw the misplaced items to me. We did this until the stairs were clean. Your stairs will willingly get cleaned and your child will giggle and have fun. They don't even realize they are cleaning. But trust me, you aren't duping them; you are simply speaking a language they comprehend, which allows you to cultivate a shift in how they get tasks done.

This is just one intervention. There is a practical, effective, and easy-to-implement play-based solution for almost every parenting challenge, and I'll give you plenty of step-by-step interventions and idea starters for how to navigate common misbehavior circumstances. *Just remember, when in doubt, play it out!*

Let me give you another example. Your child refuses to pick up their toys. Sound familiar? Yep, I've been there, too. It's time to get ready to eat dinner, you've already asked your child multiple times to clean up, and they aren't listening or following directions. You are emotionally and mentally drained and physically exhausted from taking care of your little human all day, and you just want them to comply. You've used every bribe, threat, and consequence in the book, and they don't seem to care. And the toys are still all over the floor.

You are now officially in a power struggle with your child. They are defiantly refusing to clean up, and you are starting to feel angry, resentful, and disrespected. You are about to lose it, though you're not sure if you're going to yell or cry. You need all the valor you can muster.

It is when you are at this breaking point that you need to pause and take a step back to see the entire picture before reassessing the situation. Children often have difficulty with transitions, especially when they're shifting from a preferred activity to something undesirable, such as cleaning. But don't fret! If nothing else seems to be working, that often means that play can save the day. This is the time to get it out of your head that you don't want to reward your child with play if they are misbehaving. Play is used as a communication and behavior tool at this moment, not as a reward. Play is used to speak your child's language in ways they can conceptualize and comprehend. According to Rogers and Sawyers, "Young children do not differentiate between play, learning, and work." When they engage in play, they are learning and experiencing both simultaneously. So when you use play to help you parent, not only will your children comply but you will save your sanity. Let me show you how to flip the script.

If you find yourself in this common scenario, as always, you first need to regulate your own emotions and behaviors before you can expect your child to do the same. If you are stressed and your sympathetic nervous system is triggered, you'll need to use your coping skills to come back to neutral so your brain will be able to think of play-based techniques and interventions.

Once you are calm, think, "How can I make this situation into a playful one?" Maybe you get a dump truck or grocery cart and ask your child to put all the toys inside and deliver them to the toy box before the toy factory closes for the day. Maybe you challenge them to pick up and put their toys away while they pretend to be a frog or a bunny while hopping on one foot, just to make the job a little more fun. Or maybe you challenge them to play Freeze Clean. Tell them you are going to play a game, and then put on some music and have your child clean while the music is on and freeze when the music is off. They will have so much fun they will forget they are actually cleaning, and they'll get the job done quickly—before you reach the end of the song. Trust me, it really works!

Play is an underutilized and undervalued modality and an almost secret way to parent. But it is extremely effective, and it will change your life. Are you ready to learn all my tried-and-true secrets? Buckle up, it's going to be a fun ride!

Chapter 2

How to Connect Thoughtfully and Communicate Effectively

"When you connect to the heart of a child, everything is possible."

—KARYN PURVIS

PLAY IS A VITAL PART OF A CHILD'S DEVELOPMENT AND A mechanism for parents to grow a secure attachment with their child. When play between a parent and child is purposeful, it not only strengthens the relationship but also creates a sense of safety, develops a circle of trust, and provides attunement for emotions and positive experiences. Parents are often the limit makers, rule enforcers, and consequence providers. And although boundary setting is necessary for a healthy parent-child relationship, cultivating positive interactions through play is also crucial for a child to learn what it feels like to be seen, heard, and loved.

The best way to communicate and connect with your child is through play. In this chapter, I will share common scenarios and problematic behaviors to help illustrate my theory in a relatable and palatable way. I'll also provide ways to communicate with your child playfully to enhance your connection with them.

Cultivating a Meaningful Connection with Your Child

I believe play begins between a parent and child during pregnancy. Play can really begin to take form around twenty-seven weeks in utero, when a fetus starts to hear sounds outside the body, like a parent's voice. When the fetus inside the womb starts kicking, reciprocal communication begins taking place between parent and unborn baby, play continues to develop, and core connections begin forming between them. When a parent talks, reads a book, plays music, sings aloud, and dances with their growing fetus, it builds connection through this playful communication. These are the stepping stones to grow a secure attachment, build trust, and become a safe place for your child.

Being mindful that many parents have a baby through surrogate or adoption, playful connection and communication can start at birth or as soon as the child begins living with their caregiver. That's when the parent-child attachment strengthens by the way a parent nurtures their child through loving eye contact and facial expressions, gentle sensory-based touch, and playful interactions. Through these joyful exchanges, children learn trust, safety, and emotional regulation, as well as what it feels like to be respected and honored.

And when you create a play-based connection with your child by positively and effectively communicating with them, it will also help cultivate cooperation and compliance.

Let me explain my rationale for this behavioral model. When you invest in a child's well-being by thoughtfully taking the time to listen, reflect, and validate through your words and actions, they glean a sense of connection, safety, and trust. Positive communication, verbally and nonverbally, extends an invitation to a child to be open to constructive critique and compliance requests. They know you have their best interest at heart, and they want to please you. Thus,

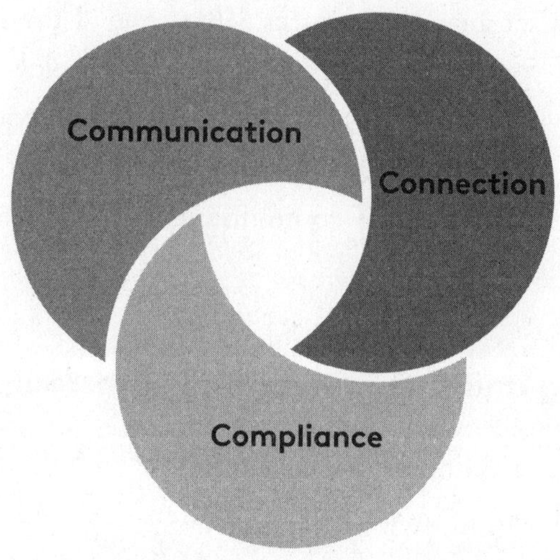

**Parenting Through Play
Behavioral Model**

they're starting from a place of positivity and openness, not resentment, defiance, and anger.

The more you positively communicate, the more securely you connect, and the more compliant the child becomes. It's a never-ending cycle of trust. Even when hardships, disagreements, and disruptions arise, the parent and child have already formed a firm foundation, a figurative safety net, and a strengthened bond that's more difficult to breach or contaminate. When this connection is nurtured and the parent and child are securely attached, the child becomes more compliant and positively behaved. There will still be power struggles, emotional dysregulation, and low frustration tolerance—we are all human, after all—but these will be less severe and the relationship will rebound more quickly when the connection is stronger.

Children thrive on connection, so it's essential for your child to have an active and obvious support system at home. Parent-child connections are formed and reinforced through contact and play that promotes sensory development. Thus, one of the best ways to connect with your child, communicate that you love them, and build a foundation of trust is through tactile stimulation and positive, playful, meaningful experiences. Let's discuss some ways to positively open the doors of communication and strengthen your connection with your child.

Connecting and Communicating with Your Child

A way parents can connect and communicate with their child effectively is by checking in with their children every day. Some children don't want to "talk" for long periods of time or don't have the speech and language skills to communicate effectively through talking. Young children are trying to find themselves and their autonomy, so it's easy to get disconnected as a parent during the younger years. If you try to have long conversations with them that sound more like a lecture, they will get irritated, restless, and withdrawn. They might even start to resent you, avoid you, and refrain from having a conversation with you. So here's my advice: Start as early as you can to build trust, and make daily check-ins a routine and an expectation. Make them effortless, quick, maybe even a little fun. This is a great way to assess your child's mood and maintain a strong connection.

Showing empathy and validation is imperative during this part of the conversation. Be careful not to overload or flood your child. Keep your reflections, questions, and supportive suggestions short and minimal. If your child doesn't want to verbalize how they are feeling on any given day, make daily check-ins playful and engaging by presenting them with a list of face emojis. Have them point to the one that best describes their mood, or have them write or draw their answers on a piece of paper. You can also have your child rate their day and/or their mood by colors. Red can mean a difficult day or an angry mood, blue can mean a sad day/mood, and yellow can mean a happy day/mood, etc.

The Daily Check-In

Ask your child to gauge their day by giving you a thumbs-up, thumbs-down, or sideways thumb, or ask them to scale their day from one to ten, depending on their developmental and cognitive level. If they give you a thumbs-up or a high number, that's great—ask them to share one positive part of their day. If it's a sideways thumb, a thumbs-down, or a low number, you can briefly follow up with a question about what went wrong and how you can support them.

Instead of talking to your child in long, drawn-out, sit-down conversations that will sound more like an excruciating lecture, try talking in small doses. Long conversations will feel suffocating, and your child is likely to feel trapped and either detach and stop listening or become irritable and act out. I think you know where this is going. A conversation that was intended to be helpful may have the opposite effect. Thus, having multiple short and to-the-point conversations instead of long lectures is much more effective.

Also, when you are having these short bursts of conversation, stay as neutral and calm as possible. If you react too quickly before methodically curating your response, you could lose your child's attention or trust. If they openly tell you about something unpleasant they heard or experienced at school, ask a curious and open-ended question like "How do you feel about that?" or "What do you think about that?" before showing concern or anger. Allow them to come up with their own thoughts and share their solutions before diving in with your own opinions and conclusions. If they say, "I need your advice," feel free to calmly share some thoughts and maybe two sides of the coin so they can thoughtfully understand the "why" behind your advice and why one decision may be better than another.

Tablet Talk

And then there are children who won't want to talk at all. How many times have you asked your child, "What's wrong?" and they reply with a shoulder shrug or a one-word answer that doesn't tell you anything? Some children feel so much pressure to "talk" to their parents if something is wrong that they disengage because it's too difficult for them to articulate their emotions for one reason or another.

I previously had a client who would regularly shut down when I met with him at his home. He would get very overwhelmed by talking face-to-face and would often hide under the couch in protest and defiantly refuse to engage with me. Even though he was very articulate, he didn't want to "talk" in the traditional way. After the first time he hid under the couch to avoid talking and participating in our session, I grabbed a play-based writing tablet that was nearby and communicated with him via notes on the tablet. I would ask questions like "What emotion are you feeling?" and provide four possible emotional responses with a box next to each one. I'd slide it under the couch with the stylus and allow him to respond. After about one minute, he pushed the tablet back out under the couch in my direction with one of the emotion boxes checked off. We play-fully exchanged this type of communication with each other a few times to keep our connection growing. Once I secured trust and safety, I wrote, "What do you want to play?" and provided him with a few options to choose from. Once the pressure to talk was no longer a threat and he felt connected and cared for, he came out from under the couch, without force or repercussion, to play with me for the remainder of the session.

Stuffed Animal Communication

In grad school we learned about a Gestalt therapy method called the Empty Chair technique, which basically allows an individual to express themselves to someone without the other person being present. It's a good way to practice how to release thoughts and emotions, as well as how to role-play having a difficult conversation with others. So of course I put my own play therapy spin on it. Instead of talking to an empty chair, I use a trusted teddy bear (honestly any stuffed animal will do) to help my own children as well as my clients strengthen communication skills and role-play difficult conversations. This is also helpful when your child refuses to talk face-to-face with you. Usually a stuffed animal works well in this scenario since it's soft and the child can squeeze it for comfort if needed during the conversation.

Once they have a stuffed animal, prompt your child and encourage them to "talk" to the stuffed animal about what's wrong, eliminating the pressure to talk to you. During this time, the parent slightly steps away or out of immediate eye contact so the child can feel free to talk to the stuffed animal without interruption. Sometimes a child wants to share without receiving any input, judgment, or feedback to externalize their thoughts and release their emotions. Typically, once a child shares what is wrong to the stuffed animal, they are more apt to share the same story with their parent later.

If your child is struggling with a peer at school or needing to advocate for themselves with a teacher or coach, this role-play exercise will help teach them how to communicate and let them practice having tough conversations. If they want, they can even speak or respond as the stuffed animal (or you can help with that part) so they see varying perspectives on how the other person could react and respond to them. They will learn what they want to say and what they don't. They can practice as long as they need to before having the conversation in real life. A child can also use a handheld mirror for a similar effect.

Puppets and Play Phones

Researchers conclude that puppets are one of the most valuable tools in working with children because they are innately appealing and lend themselves to a range of theoretical approaches of play therapy (Reynolds and Stanley 2001). Puppets also serve to help children express what they have trouble verbalizing. Let me share an example. One afternoon I was upset about something and was crying. When my son saw me, he grabbed one of my play therapy puppets and brought it to me in an effort to help me feel better. He didn't have to use any words. I knew he was using the puppet to connect with me and communicate that he loved me and I wasn't alone. A few days later, he was sad about something and walked over to me with a different puppet from my play bin. He said, "Elephant needs a hug," because he was trying to connect with me and communicate to me that *he* needed a hug. My children teach me so much about play.

On the clinical side, years ago I had a client who was very emotionally distraught because her parents were recently divorced and she had moved away from one of her parents. She wouldn't talk to anyone about it, even me. Every time I asked her about her estranged parent, she would change the subject and ignore the question. So one day I brought out my animal puppets, who quickly became her trusted friends. After a few sessions, one of the animals asked her about her estranged parent, and she immediately opened up and shared all her feelings with the animal puppet, who continued to ask questions and receive enthusiastic responses. Talking to the puppet helped the child feel safe (even though I was the one controlling the puppet) and allowed her to open up about this sensitive subject to her animal friend, even though I was physically sitting right there. It was all about the play and the connection. You can also use two puppets—one for you and one for your child—to have a conversation together. In this scenario, the puppets "talk" to each other. There is a level of separation, which helps the child feel at ease to communicate. The parent receives the information they need in a trusting and playful way.

In a later session, this same client used my play telephone to call her estranged parent to say that she missed them. She proceeded to call this parent during subsequent sessions to share about her day. Despite their absence from one another, this little girl craved communication, connection, and play with her parent. For a similar effect, get two play telephones and call each other to "talk it out." This way your child doesn't feel the pressure of an intimidating conversation filled with eye contact and big words. You can even be in separate rooms as long as you can both hear each other clearly. This physical separation during the "talk" helps a child stay connected to you and also feel comfortable enough to discuss the matter at hand playfully.

Sand Tray

Another play-based way to get your children to open up and communicate their emotions is through a sand tray. All a parent needs is a little dirt from the backyard or a small bin with sand in it, along with a few toy figurines, miniature cars, or toys from around the house. Once all the materials are gathered, the parent asks the child to use the figures in the sand to tell them a story about their day or show them why they are upset. Through play, the parent is present, attentive, and quiet. If a child desires an interactive response, a parent can share reflective statements of what the child is showing in their story. In most cases, the story is demonstrated in the play and the parent is told what is wrong without the child even having to say a word. This is a safe way for the child to communicate and express themselves. It is also a way for the child to feel connected to their parent on a deeper level through play. Once the child is done sharing their story, the parent can ask how they can be supportive. The child might just want a hug, or they might want advice or feedback. The parent then honors their child's choice as a way to continue the trust and secure attachment between them.

Listen to Your Child Without Invalidating Them

When a child shares a story or experience about their day or something they are struggling with, practice listening and not responding. We don't like to see our children in any pain and innately want to help them. But sometimes we interject our advice based on our own similar stories and experiences. We intend to relate to them, but in actuality this invalidates the child and they become resentful, angry, or withdrawn.

Even though you could have a parallel experience as your child's, you have to remember that when we compare stories, it pivots the focus from them to you, and that can feel invalidating. Even though it may be a similar experience, it's not the same experience. You may not truly be able to understand your child's unique perspective and how they are conceptualizing the experience. When your child says, "You just don't understand," the truth is, you may not. If this is you, say, "Help me understand in your words. I may not understand, and I'd like to."

Allow them to have their moment, and just be there to hold space and listen. As parents we tend to be problem solvers and don't give children many choices. You can still show empathy by saying, "That must be hard. I had a similar experience and know a bit how you might feel." Then ask, "Do you want me to just listen or help you solve the problem?" In the moment of distress, they may not know how to respond, so just continue to listen.

The most important element of this process is learning how to pause before you respond—it's the most powerful and helpful way to connect and support your child. It's our role as parents to empower our children to learn what they need and share how we can best support them.

A relationship built on communication is about understanding and empowering children. Sometimes they just need to express themselves and externalize the problem. By helping them solve their own problems, you are teaching them that you trust them and believe in their decision-making skills. This will help children become better critical thinkers and grow up to feel confident and less indecisive. In the heat of the emotion, our children don't need us to problem-solve, they need us to hear and attend to their emotion and experience. Once you do that, they may come back and want to talk through problem-solving.

Practice "I" Statements

Teach your children how to use "I" statements: For example, "I feel rejected when you say you can't play with me. Instead of ignoring me or saying no without any explanation, I'd prefer you say something like, 'I would love to spend time with you because I know it's important to you. I can't play right now, so let's play after dinner instead.'" When you communicate together using "I" statements, it helps both the parent and child become less defensive when discussing difficult emotions.

Mailbox Masterpieces

Want a fun way to nonverbally communicate with your child that is innovative, effective, and playful? Get out a piece of paper and some crayons, and ask your child to draw a story about how they are feeling or what is wrong. Go a step further and set up a mailbox, paper or sticky notes, and a writing implement in a place in the house that is reachable and visible to both of you. Then you can exchange notes or drawings in the mailbox, depending on your child's age.

Play Charades

This charades game focuses on acting out emotions, thoughts, and behaviors. Those are the three categories you should concentrate on when playing with your child. You can take turns acting out what is frustrating them or how they are feeling, then find solutions to the problem being presented. This is a fun way to nonverbally communicate with your child in an effective and playful way.

Connecting and Communicating with Less Yelling and More Nurturing

Let's talk for a moment about raising our voices when communicating with our children. When a parent starts looking at yelling through a different lens and understands that raising their voice and angrily handing out threats and punishments can be damaging and detrimental to the child's mental well-being, they begin to realize that they can parent through challenging situations more effectively with nurturing connection and patience instead.

If a child doesn't feel safe with their parent or lacks trust and security, their connection is broken, and the child will act out. If a child feels safe and supported, the parent and child will have a stronger connection, and behavior outcomes will be more positive. Yelling doesn't solve any parenting dilemma or child behavior. It may startle a child into complying in the moment, so it may appear effective to parents who raise their voice at their child, but yelling has long-term detriments to a child's mental health and won't ultimately correct a child's behavior.

The Brain–Behavior Connection

"Scientists have discovered that it takes approximately 400 repetitions to create a new synapse in the brain, unless it is done in play, in which case it only takes 10 to 20 repetitions."

—KARYN PURVIS

I acknowledge that we, as parents, are all human, and adulting can be very challenging at times. And I think it's safe to assume that the vast majority of us have lost our temper at some point and yelled at our children in the heat of the moment. What's more, if your child is young, their brain is still developing and they will inevitably get into trouble at some point, whether they try to or not. They are still learning about the world, cause and effect, and right from wrong. It's our job to guide, coach, and teach them, and hopefully being reminded of this gives us perspective when they do misbehave. They aren't necessarily acting out to be defiant or disrespectful. Sometimes they do it because it's a cry for help; other times they just didn't use their prefrontal cortex to think through their actions.

The prefrontal cortex is responsible for controlling our executive functioning, including thinking, problem-solving, predicting consequences, and decision-making. It also helps regulate emotions, control impulses, and conceptualize how our behaviors in the moment affect our future. The prefrontal cortex isn't fully developed until a person is about twenty-five years old, so our five-year-olds have twenty years to perfect these skills. Before the prefrontal cortex is fully developed, a child uses and depends on a part of the brain called the amygdala, the emotional part of our brain that tends to lead children to impulsive decisions, emotional dysregulation, and risky behaviors. If you're reading this and a light bulb just flashed in your head, you aren't the only one. When I share this knowledge with other parents, they are typically wowed by it. When a parent understands how a child's brain develops and works, they tend to have more patience and understanding for their child's behavior.

Karyn Purvis created the attachment-based Trust-Based Relational Intervention (TBRI®) model, which emphasizes that learning through play enables the brain to form new connections more effectively because it reduces stress and engages emotions. According to the Karyn Purvis Institute of Child Development at Texas Christian University, this model is widely used to support children with complex trauma, adversity, early harm, abuse, neglect, and toxic stress because it focuses on building trust and creating a safe environment to cultivate growth and healing. While the model is based on years of attachment, sensory processing, and neuroscience research, the foundation of TBRI is connection.

Researchers at the institute have concluded that play-based learning can activate the brain's reward pathways, promoting synaptic growth much faster than rote repetition. By emphasizing and fostering play-based interactions, this model focuses on the plasticity of the brain to nurture emotional growth in children who have experienced stress, adversity, and trauma. So when we are trying to get our children to listen, comply, and behave, communicating that to them in a play-based way is more effective than yelling, shaming, threatening, and punishing.

Teaching Empathy and Making a Repair

The most well-educated, well-intentioned parent can be susceptible to yelling at their child from time to time. I get it. I've been there, too. I yell more when I am exhausted, overwhelmed, or over-stimulated. First, address your own triggers, then spend time self-reflecting to find the core of your yelling. When dysregulated, pause before engaging with your child. Emotions can run pretty high at times, and after a long day of mental and emotional stimulation, it's not easy to manage them. An occasional slip won't severely harm your child, especially if you can make a repair with them. Yelling from time to time can, in fact, show your child that you are a human being and can make mistakes once in a while. Making a repair, apologizing, and taking responsibility for your behaviors not only will help strengthen your connection, it's also healing for both parent and child. Teach your child that no one is perfect, and that you and they are alike.

After an angry exchange between parent and child, a repair is often recommended. A repair is a process to resolve conflict with a goal of mending the relationship. When a child does something to hurt or harm their parent, sibling, or peer, they can learn how to make a repair with others from the parent role-modeling this process. Something similar, called restorative practice, is used in schools. Restorative practice is typically defined as a method to restore a positive connection, acknowledging hurt emotions and working toward rebuilding trust and a secure attachment. Here's how it works:

- Role-model and practice emotional regulation coping skills with your child.
- Acknowledge behaviors with your child by writing/drawing/saying an apology to the person/s they hurt. Role-model empathy and normalize imperfection.
- Reflect with your child about what they could have done differently.

However, I would like to add that you should never force a child to apologize. Instead, focus on humility and empathy. This is a teaching moment to reflect and respond. You shouldn't invalidate, shame, or punish your child for refusing to apologize on your terms. If a child harmed you or someone else, they need to learn how their behaviors and actions affect others, the natural consequences or outcomes of their actions and behaviors, and how to humbly come to a peaceful resolution if they made a mistake. Sometimes we, parents and children included, hurt someone's feelings without intending to, and it's better to teach humility rather than defensiveness.

When someone has empathy, they are able to actively value another person's perspective and respond with care and concern. It is important to teach children to listen to how others are feeling and then reflect on how they are feeling. Young children tend to be in their egocentric era, so empathy doesn't come naturally to them. And if a child doesn't know a multitude of emotions or isn't able to freely express emotions in their home, they may have a more difficult time being empathetic, showing compassion, or considering someone else's perspective.

Here is an example of an empathy script to help identify behaviors, reflect on emotions, and teach boundaries, compassionate repair, and peaceful resolution.

Child 1 pulls toy away from their sibling.
Child 2 starts crying and tries to hit their sibling.
Parent: How did it make [your sibling] feel when you took
their toy away?
Child 1: It made them feel mad and sad.
Parent: That's a good observation. Is that how you'd feel if it
happened to you?
Child 1: Yes. It would hurt my feelings and make me angry.
Parent: What can you do now?
Child 1: Say I'm sorry and give the toy back.
Parent: That would be kind. What can you do differently
next time?
Child 1: Ask for the toy nicely instead of taking it away.

If yelling and apologizing becomes a regular routine loop, a pattern of yelling and apologizing like a broken record, there is a larger problem at play. The repair doesn't become your get-out-of-jail-free card. A parent shouldn't depend on a repair or use it frequently, or it will lose value. I'm not saying you have to be a Zen-like, mellow, gentle parent all the time. That is unrealistic, even for the calmest among us. It's the humble, positive communication and connection that takes place after an emotionally charged moment that can help repair a relationship. The chronic yelling can sever the connection between a parent and child, and some parents have a lower frustration tolerance than other parents. Yelling alone can be cathartic, and I sometimes encourage it when a child or parent is in distress, but I don't condone yelling at another person.

We are in control of our emotions and accountable for our behaviors. If I impulsively raise my voice at my child, I am instantly riddled with shame, guilt, and regret. When a parent says a child deserves that type of response, I do not agree. That response is more about the parent and their emotional needs than it is about the child. Sure, our children can behave in some challenging ways sometimes, but even then, it doesn't warrant reacting out of anger, retaliation, pettiness, or manipulating the child's emotional state by giving them the silent treatment. Remember, you are the adult. Your brain is fully functional and developed, your child's isn't. You aren't role-modeling emotional regulation by reacting in anger, and you aren't solving a problem by yelling at them. Yelling at your child means you are out of control, not in control.

In fact, what you are doing is causing short- and long-term damage to their development as well as to their emotional and mental well-being. Research studies have shown time and time again that yelling at your child can trigger a fight-or-flight stress response in their brain, which leads to heightened anxiety. Let's talk about this for a moment.

If a child is constantly living in a state of heightened anxiety, there can be some serious side effects. The fight-or-flight response is a physiological reaction to a perceived threat that affects our sympathetic nervous system, and it plays a critical role in how our bodies deal with stress and how we perceive a dangerous situation or problematic setting. When we are threatened by a person or an unsafe environment, this innate and automatic survival response can help us prepare for and perform under intense pressure. This is a defense mechanism that can actually help us survive effectively if we are in danger. The fight-or-flight response can also cause hormonal changes, increased heart rate, high blood pressure, a spike in blood sugar, and muscle tension or trembling.

If both parent and child are experiencing this type of acute stress response simultaneously, there will not be positive outcomes. When a child is consistently living in this survival state, they are more likely to respond to their world and the people in it irritably and aggressively because their cortisol levels are consistently high. Thus they are responding emotionally, not rationally. They respond impulsively because they are dysregulated, which causes their behavior to worsen. Yelling becomes a trigger if it happens often enough. You'll know this is the case if you raise your voice and your child immediately runs and hides or bursts into tears. In addition to behavioral responses, long-term exposure to this type of heightened stress can be harmful to a child's physical health. Chronic stress can lead to an increased risk of anxiety; depression; gastrointestinal issues; headaches; heart attack or stroke; metabolic disorders, such as diabetes and obesity; high blood pressure and cholesterol; poor immune function; reproductive and sexual dysfunction; and asthma.

The Fight-or-Flight Response

To help understand how our children react in the moment, it might be helpful to review the phases of the fight-or-flight response:

The Alarm Phase: The central nervous system is activated and begins to prepare your body to stay or sprint.

The Resistance Phase: The body and brain are trying to regulate and return to baseline or pre-arousal level, which can take roughly twenty to sixty minutes.

The Exhaustion Phase: When chronically experienced, this phase can cause physical, mental, and emotional exhaustion.

According to a *Child Development* article titled "Longitudinal Links Between Fathers' and Mothers' Harsh Verbal Discipline and Adolescents' Conduct Problems and Depressive Symptoms" (Wang and Kenny 2013), when a child is chronically yelled at, it can result in increased maladaptive behavior challenges, lower self-image, and more depression. The study focused primarily on harsh verbal discipline from parents, including yelling, name-calling, insults, mocking, criticism, and shaming, which can lead to feelings of worthlessness and inferiority. On the flip side, the authors concluded that if a parent shows concern, comfort, affection, and responsiveness to their child, this emotional connectedness will increase a child's desire to communicate with their parents and decrease problem behaviors. Furthermore, according to Grusec and Goodnow's (1994) research, when a parent and child have a trusted and loving relationship, the child may not react negatively to discipline but instead will adopt the values and behaviors presented by their parents.

If your yelling triggers a fear or stress response in your child, there might be a problem. Chronic yelling at a child can cause more than fear and anxiety. It can also cause anger, resentment, rebellion, low grades, aggression, low self-esteem, and depression. Worse yet, it defuses the behavior you are seeking from your child, which is the opposite of your intentions. When you continually yell at a child to defuse their behavior, they will eventually become desensitized and shut down. Some studies have shown that chronic yelling at children can cause physical symptoms as well, such as headaches, stomachaches, and even chronic pain later in life. Furthermore, yelling at a child that involves shame, threats, punishments, and any emotional or verbal abuse can result in the child becoming a bully to others. Saying things like "I'll give you something to cry about" or "If you do ____ again, I will ____" is threatening to a child and triggers a detrimental stress response, not one that will signal to them to never misbehave again. Parents yell to feel in control when they are out of control. Yelling doesn't command compliance or positive behavior. It perpetuates the behavior you are trying to defuse.

We should be teaching children that they need to learn from their mistakes and believe they are ultimately good. They should be taught what the right choice is, given the opportunity to put it into practice, and encouraged when they behave in a positive way. They need support, validation, and empathy. I'm not saying they should never have limits or a consequence if they do something wrong, it just should be handled without yelling, shaming, punishments, criticisms, or threats. The best thing you can do for your child is to be patient, calm, and in control, as well as emotionally regulated. Connect with them by being a good listener, empathizing with them, and validating their experience. Help them feel valued, respected, seen, heard, and securely loved. And allow them to feel empowered by your support. It's imperative that parents intentionally and positively communicate, connect, and play with their children to nurture their relationship and develop a more meaningful connection. If a child feels connected and securely attached to their parent, behavior concerns appear to be less drastic, cultivating a more peaceful home. Then, when a power struggle surfaces or compliance is requested, the child is more inclined to behave positively without protest.

Chapter 3

The Power of Play: When in Doubt, Play It Out!

> "Play is our brain's favorite way of learning."
>
> —Diane Ackerman

I BELIEVE PLAY CAN TRANSFORM A FAMILY'S LIFE AND IS the best medicine for many of our daily challenges. We have been programmed to think that we shouldn't play when we are upset. Who has time to think about playing when they are angry or overwhelmed, or especially when their child is misbehaving? Play is what you do when you are happy or as a reward when you complete a task or have been well behaved, right? Let's challenge that thought.

I recall having a client years ago at an elementary school. The teacher of this child, despite signed authorization from the school and the parents, refused to let the child leave her class to see me for brief weekly therapy sessions. I will never forget the teacher telling me that she didn't think the child should leave to go play with me when she had just been misbehaving in class. The teacher believed that going to see me for therapy was a reward and that the child didn't deserve to play. She was under the impression that the child should behave in class and earn the right to see me for therapeutic support. What that teacher couldn't understand was that our weekly therapy sessions were helping the child with her behavior, and denying her that opportunity was making the child's behavior worse. I ended up involving the principal and was eventually able to see the child regularly. Her behavior in the classroom improved. Play was in fact not a reward but ultimately a solution.

The concept of a parent shifting to a Play-It-Out modality with their child when a problematic situation occurs is a new and unique parenting style that I live by, shifting from a traditional punishment style to a modern play style to modify behavior. Garry Landreth (2002) says, "For children to 'play out' their experiences and feelings is the most natural, dynamic, and self-healing process in which they can engage" (p. 13).

This chapter will educate you on the importance, benefits, and therapeutic powers of play. But before we get into how influential play can be, let me discuss the tenets of play therapy, to show you what a powerful yet very underutilized tool it can be in transforming a child's mental health and behavior.

The Benefits of Parenting Through Play

In an article published in *Pediatrics* titled "The Importance of Play in Promoting Healthy Child Development and Maintaining Strong Parent-Child Bonds" (Ginsburg et al. 2007), the authors concluded that "play is essential to development because it contributes to the cognitive, physical, social, and emotional well-being of children and youth. Play also offers an ideal opportunity for parents to engage fully with their children."

I want to take a moment to reflect on the importance on the timing of this article for me. It was published in the same year I started graduate school to earn my PsyD. I hadn't yet taken a play therapy course, but for some reason I find significance in the fact that my book comes full-circle with this article. This quote, in my opinion, embodies the essence of this book. By the time this book is written, published, and on bookshelves, that article will be almost twenty years old yet still widely relevant to our current parenting culture. Its principles and findings have been studied for over twenty years, yet play-based parenting is still not a mainstream parenting method. That is why I wholeheartedly believe in what this book can do to help parents see the value of play and understand how play-based parenting can result in a better relationship with their children and a more peaceful home.

The authors begin by stating, "Play is so important to optimal child development that it has been recognized by the United Nations High Commission for Human Rights as a right of every child." As Rogers and Sawyers (1988) stated, "Play is the essence of life and is perhaps the only human behavior that integrates and balances all aspects of human functioning." Levy (1978), too, concluded that "play is an active form of learning that unites the mind, body, and spirit."

Jonathan Haidt, author of *The Anxious Generation* (2024), states, "Play is the work of childhood, and all young mammals have the same job: Wire up your brain by playing vigorously and often" (p. 51). He goes on to say, "Hundreds of studies on young rats, monkeys, and humans show that young mammals want to play, need to play, and come out socially, cognitively, and emotionally impaired when they are deprived of play" (p. 52).

The Power of Connecting Through Play

Play is a universal behavior and an expression of thoughts and feelings in children. A child's development and parental connection are strongly influenced by loving relationships and how parents effectively and consistently relate to their children through play.

When parents play with their child, whether they are passively observing or actively engaging, they get a front-row seat to how their children view the world and how they make sense of it. When a parent is present during play experiences, it invites them to fully engage with their child and cultivate the connection between them, which builds a stronger bond and an enduring relationship. Through play, parents are gifted the opportunity to learn how to more effectively communicate with their child and provide nurturing guidance.

Since children are often allowed the freedom to express themselves through play, parents can observe their perspective, thoughts, and emotions. This insight allows parents to support their children because they learn how to speak the child's language. This is helpful because so many children are expected to learn the parent's language, which often leads to communication barriers and cutoffs. Play also offers a softness to almost any situation, and the more a parent is enthusiastic about their child's play, the more the child will feel confident and competent in their play, encouraging a healthy self-esteem. Your interest, encouragement, and response to their play matters.

The interaction between a child's challenges and their families is always complex. Within the context of play therapy, researchers conclude that children and families heal faster when they work—and play—together. How a family plays together becomes an important part of a child's learning and healing processes (A4PT, n.d.). And in my experience as a play therapist combined with my experience as a mom, I've seen that when play is practiced with a parent and child simultaneously, better outcomes arise, benefiting both.

The Benefits of Play

Play is a fun, enjoyable activity that elevates our spirits and brightens our outlook on life. It expands self-expression, self-knowledge, self-actualization, self-advocacy, and self-efficacy (A4PT, n.d.). Play connects us to others in a positive way, stimulates creative thinking and exploration, and regulates our emotions (Landreth 2002).

Children understand play and respond to play-based communication more than to any other modality. Not only does play serve as a mechanism for children to learn communication skills, language skills, and social skills, it also affects their behavior. Through play, children learn to communicate with others, express feelings, modify behavior, build confidence and resilience, master skills, share, take turns, and develop critical problem-solving skills (A4PT, n.d.). Play is also instrumental in helping children alleviate stress, relieve boredom, and learn core strategies on how to resolve conflict.

Play is a fundamental way for children to express themselves, and it allows children the freedom to discover who they are. Without saying a word, a child can create an imaginary world for themselves and get lost in their own space. Take a moment to observe your children as they play—it will amaze you.

The Stages of Play

According to Piaget's developmental stages of play, this is how children typically play, depending on their age and developmental level.

- Practice Play: Birth to twelve months (sensory)
- Construction Play: Twelve to twenty-four months (building and categorizing)
- Symbolic Play: Two to six years (imagination and roles)
- Game Play: Seven years and older (games with rules)

The Tenets of Play Therapy

Play therapy is a way of honoring and helping children based on their unique developmental level, using play as a communication tool. It is about establishing trust, safety, respect, and acceptance for a child, and as such it can be used to help them cope with difficult emotions and find solutions to problems (Reddy et al. 2005). Play therapy also allows children to change the way they think about, feel toward, and resolve their concerns (Russ and Kaugars 2001). Research supports the effectiveness of play therapy with children experiencing a wide variety of social, emotional, behavioral, and learning challenges (A4PT, n.d.).

Knowing the value of play therapy is extremely useful in helping parents understand how they can honor their children through a play therapy lens. Virginia Axline contributed eight basic principles for play therapy in her work as one of the legendary founders of the field. Although a therapist's relationship with a child will be different from that of a parent, some of her principles can be applied to parenthood and how a parent shows up and responds to their child. A play therapist should be warm and friendly, cultivating a positive relationship with the child and accepting them as they are. A play therapist also allows the child to freely express themselves and reflect back to them in a nonjudgmental manner. A play therapist maintains a deep respect for the child's ability to solve their own problems and leaves the responsibility to make choices and institute change to the child.

If a parent can relate to their child in a similar manner as a therapist would, it could result in better behavior, improved communication and understanding, and ultimately a healthier relationship.

Why Play Isn't Prioritized in the Home

With budgets being cut from schools and playtime being minimized, children aren't receiving adequate time to play in that setting. And with our own hectic parenting schedules these days, many children aren't getting enough opportunities for play at home, either. I don't think it's a stretch to conclude that play isn't prioritized in the home as much as it was years ago because of the rise of technology. Technology-driven entertainment like television, tablets, video games, the Internet, computer-based gaming, and social media consume a lot of our time and engagement throughout the day. It's hard to compete with technology.

Play is also minimized in the home because parents are exhausted and are competing with a mental load greater than ever before. Parents often go into toxic productivity mode and forget to slow down to rest or play. Schedules are overbooked and parents dismiss the importance of play. It becomes an afterthought as chores, homework, errands, sports, and after-school commitments take over.

In my home, I carve out decompression time following a long day, an extended outing, a vacation, or even regularly after school. We have decompression time before I place additional demands of the day on my children. I used to make sure chores and homework were done as soon as we got home from school, but I quickly realized that my children needed downtime in the afternoon before I could expect them to perform at their best after a fast-paced day. Decompression time usually lasts for thirty to sixty minutes, and it's a time when my children can decompress in a way that is helpful to them, whether it is playing outside, relaxing in their room, reading, drawing, crafting, or just zoning out. I try to limit screens during this time, especially because it can overstimulate a child and produce the opposite effect of what I am striving for, but if it's a slow-paced show that helps them rest their body and brain, I allow it from time to time.

There are also many movement videos available that can be helpful during this time if that type of sensory stimulation is what your child needs. Not every child needs the lights down and soft music to relax—some children, in fact, need the opposite. This is a time to allow space for your child to rest and rejuvenate before you expect them to deliver or perform. If you don't give them a break, you run the risk of emotional dysregulation and more power struggles.

There is also a phenomenon called the professionalization of parenthood, which tends to create guilt in parents who find it challenging to "balance competing demands after a taxing workday" (Ginsberg et al.) This is when play becomes a chore and not an organic way to relieve stress or strengthen the bond between parent and child. Planning less and providing ample opportunities to play and interact with our child may actually cultivate less stress and make us more effective parents.

Many children thrive on routine, structure, and schedules, and are inspired and motivated by involvement in school and other community activities and projects. However, if it's not balanced, a pressured and hurried lifestyle typically is a source of emotional dysregulation, stress, and anxiety. I try not to schedule more than one activity each day, and I leave some days open. This balance is difficult to achieve, especially if you have multiple children with multiple interests outside the home. Despite outside pressures to achieve physically, academically, and socially, parents need to remember that personal downtime is vital for a child's healthy development. We also don't want to limit our children and face understimulation—there is a balance, and it is different for every child and every family. Be active, but also know when it's time to rest or play.

Invitation to Play

Do you create opportunities to play throughout the day? Are toys, crafts, art supplies, and other play-based activities readily available to your children?

In my home, if ready-made activities aren't in my children's reach but tucked away in a forgotten room or cabinet, my children and

I will neglect them. I am not suggesting leaving toys all over your home, but I do recommend having a basket with some toys, stuffed animals, art supplies, books, puzzles, and other activities available for your child to see and grab at a moment's notice, and ideally without your help. The more independent they are in choosing their play, the better, plus that means you don't have to stop what you are doing in that moment and fetch them supplies, materials, and other items. On that note, children do not need toys to play. Their imagination can take them a long way. Give them a box, tape, markers, or some sticks and rocks, and they can come up with a whole slew of games and ideas on how to have fun.

I suggest having an invitation-to-play basket near the kitchen or family room so you can see your child play but can also do other tasks nearby, like cook dinner or sit and read a book. A lot of times my own children will automatically default to watching a screen of some kind, not because they actually prefer to but because they forget about other play-based options or it seems too difficult to think of an idea from scratch and gather all the supplies to play what they want. As parents we need to make it easier for them by front-loading the opportunity for them.

Letting Kids Be Kids

I was recently telling a friend about my daughter's eleventh birthday party, and she said, "That's a beautiful illustration of play. You should put that in your book!" My daughter is at the age where she is changing from little kid to big kid and constantly struggles with the in-between feeling. I believe children of all coming-of-age moments experience this, whether it's from baby to toddler, toddler to preschooler, elementary school to middle school, and so on. There is a pull they feel from both sides, and they experience both identities at the same time until they eventually go fully to their new identity. This was so apparent at my daughter's birthday party. All the children were dressed up in fancy clothes, trying to look and feel a little older than they really were, but instead of being too cool for their age in front of their peers, something magical happened. These "big kids" started to play a game of tag in the middle of the party. They didn't care what they looked like or how old they were—they threw off their shoes and ran around barefoot, laughing the entire time. It was my favorite part of the party and made my heart so happy to know they still had it in them. Even at their age, play was still a priority for these little kids in big kid bodies.

I believe older children and adults struggle with this as well. We tend to think that by the time we reach a particular age, play isn't appropriate anymore. We care too much about what others think about us, and we convince ourselves that play is just for little kids and that it's socially not appropriate to play after a certain age.

How Stress Starves Play

Unlike most children, adults forget to play when they are stressed. When our cups are overpoured and our schedules are overfilled with a million things we need to do, we tend to block the part of our brain that signals us to play. Play gets put on the back burner and is relegated from our lives.

In addition to not leaving ourselves enough unscheduled time throughout our day, we tend to use coping skills other than play when we are stressed. These might include drinking more coffee, having a cocktail, scrolling on our phone, or zoning out in front of the TV. Healthier and more positive coping options might include going for a walk or a run, journaling, meditation, or reading a book. But most adult coping skills don't usually include play. After all, how can a parent who is being pushed to the brink think about play?

Creative growth, reflection, and play are often neglected when we're stressed. Play becomes a burden. It is thought of as work. Play isn't spontaneous at that point; it needs to be planned out. But what if play was the answer to your stress? Do you think you would prioritize it? Would you start planning it into your day? Do you think you would play more?

Action Step: Close your eyes for a moment and picture a semi-perfect day. The sun is shining, but it's not too warm and there is a slight breeze. You don't have a lot to do. The major tasks of the day are completed, and you're in a positive mood. You are calmly sitting on your patio, smiling from ear to ear because your child is happy, content, and playing freely in the backyard. You barely have to parent, and your child is living their best life, which means you are living your best life. Everyone is having a low-stress day filled with unstructured play activities. You say to yourself, "We should do this more. This feels good." And then life happens, and poof, you don't have a day like this again for weeks, maybe months. You know these days exist because you have lived them, but you often don't think of cultivating a day like this in your schedule. Rather, this day is viewed as a fluke, a special treat, a happenstance. But it doesn't have to be. This day wasn't a mistake or an accident. This day didn't happen by chance or extreme circumstance. Maybe it happened unexpectedly because you didn't plan it, but I assure you, it wasn't a stroke of luck. I often hear parents say, "I have too much to do today; we don't have time to play." To them, play isn't something that has to get done, so it's a special treat when it happens. I challenge you to shift that mentality. Start believing that play can cultivate more peace and joy in your life if you allow it.

Chapter 4

The ABCs of Behavior

"The important thing is to teach a child that good can always triumph over evil."

—Walt Disney

THIS CHAPTER IS ABOUT LEARNING HOW TO IDENTIFY THE motivation behind your child's behavior so you can come up with effective solutions and positive outcomes. Although there are many factors that can contribute to a child's behavior, in this chapter I outline the most common underlying reasons why children misbehave and how to gain insight into how they behave. Keep in mind that children don't go out of their way to misbehave or upset their caregivers. In fact, research has shown that children innately want to perform well and make their parents happy. There is often a specific reason for why they are behaving a certain way.

A: Avoidance

The first reason children may misbehave is they want to avoid a person or task. This could mean pretending to be sick so they can avoid going to school because they don't like their teacher or a bully. This could also mean they might pick a fight with a classmate at recess to get sent to the principal's office so they get out of taking their math test. They might throw a fit before bath time because they want to keep playing or tell you how much they dislike you just to be sent to their room so they can play instead of eating their vegetables. When this happens, try to be a detective and find out what your child is attempting to avoid. Remember, the answer isn't always on the surface. It may be hidden, but the behavior is often predictable and can be found with enough mindful tracking. Once you find the reason for the behavior and what your child is trying to avoid, have an open, nonjudgmental conversation with them about it. Your child is avoiding a task because they feel they have no other choice. Find a solution to the problem together.

B: Boredom

A second reason children may misbehave is that they are bored. In reality, a little boredom is good for a child's soul and is often a time that can evoke creativity and imaginative play. But if a child is left alone for a long period of time without any type of physical movement or intellectual stimulation, they might act out because of boredom. When children are bored, they seek their own stimulation, which can sometimes mean getting into mischief. There is typically no harmful intent to their behavior when boredom is the reason, but it is still a prominent reason why children can misbehave. When this happens, pay attention to how much movement and activity they have had that day. Then ask yourself how much attention you've given them that day. Do you need to set up a game or an arts and craft table for them? Do they need a backyard play break to run around and get some fresh air? Look at your day objectively and find a way to give your child a task or change up the scenery for them.

C: Connection

A third reason children may misbehave is because they feel emotionally neglected and disconnected from their caregiver. If they are feeling lonely, insecure, or a variety of other tender emotions, they may act out to get your attention and may not always do it in a positive way. This may look like crying, having a tantrum, or picking an argument, all because they want you to pay attention to them. They are seeking connection and don't always have the words, language, or courage to say, "I am sad and need you right now." Thus, the maladaptive behaviors start occurring. When this happens, I recommend setting a designated time to spend with your child without technology or distractions. Really listen to them and be present and validate their needs. A little intentional one-on-one time goes a long way.

Power

A fourth reason children may misbehave is over a power struggle. If a child isn't feeling heard, respected, empowered, or validated, they often resort to fighting for some sort of power and control, even if that means misbehaving. When this happens, it is a sign to parents to rip off the bandage and find what is cut deep down inside. Needing power might stem from feeling like something in their life is unpredictable and out of control. They are seeking some sort of empowerment, predictability, and control. Take a moment to find out how they can feel heard, empowered, respected, and validated. This may mean that a parent needs to swallow some pride and let go of some control. It also might mean that a child is going through a developmental stage where they need more independence. This is the time to find ways to help them feel autonomous. Perhaps you could give them a task to do that you usually do for them. Or maybe ask them what is fair and let them have a say on how many vegetables to eat, what time they go to bed, or how much time is spent with technology. Compromise and negotiate. And remember what it was like to be a child, being told what to do by every adult in your life. A little goes a long way. Trust me, fewer arguments occur when this extra step is taken.

What Is Your Child's Motivation?

Oftentimes we can notice a pattern when our child misbehaves. Here are the most common reasons for a child's misbehavior.

Lack of Basic Needs

What have they eaten today? Have they drunk enough water? Do they need a snack? Are they eating a well-balanced diet? Are they getting sick? Do they feel well? Have you taken their temperature? Do they need to rest? What time did they go to bed last night? Are they waking up a lot through the night? Are they getting enough sleep?

Emotional Reactivity

Did they get a bad grade on a test? Did they watch something scary on TV? Has a sad memory been triggered? Was someone mean to them at school? Did they fall while playing outside? Did you say no to them? Did you deny them access to something? Did they just get in trouble for something they did?

Life Change

Did you just move? Do they have a new sibling? Did their pet fish just die? Did you just give their toys to Goodwill? Even if you think it is a little change, for them it can be magnified. They may be trying to make sense of it all and adjust accordingly.

Let's Get Curious

Sometimes children have multiple reasons why they act out. And when I say act out, I don't always mean a full-blown meltdown with kicking and screaming on the floor. Sometimes children are more subtle about their behavior. Children can show minor irritation about something, be extra picky at mealtime, or whine about something that may typically not bother them.

Let me share a little story about my children to illustrate. We were recently at a theme park, and near the end of the day, my children wanted one last ride before we planned to head home. Since this ride had a contained line and my children were old enough to ride without my husband and me, we gave them autonomy to responsibly ride on their own with some safety rules. I had asked them to stay together at all times and instructed my daughter to take care of her younger brother. They were very excited to go on a ride as "big kids" without their parents, while me and my husband sat on a bench near the line where we could visually see them the entire time.

After the ride was done, my natural first question was how things went in line. My daughter told me that halfway through the longer-than-expected line, her younger brother started to whine, saying he was tired and bored and wanted to come back to my husband and me. I was so proud of her for not panicking and missing out on a ride I know they both loved.

Instead, she made waiting in the line a game for him. She gave the other people they were in line with a fictitious name and role in their imaginative story. As they moved along slowly in line, they playfully created an entire story made up of the characters around them. I almost burst out in tears of joy as I praised her for using a play-based technique to keep her brother engaged in line. She could have easily gotten annoyed and frustrated by his whining, but instead, she quickly thought outside the box and engaged him through play.

After we finished our conversation, she asked me if I was going to put this technique she created in my book, and of course I said yes!

Sometimes it doesn't take much. Play-based techniques can be simple and can be done anywhere under the majority of circumstances with most children. Next time you feel stuck, think of how to handle it from a child's point of view, engage your child through play, and see the magic happen.

Now let's look at other functions of behavior that may provoke a child to misbehave.

Tangible (Denial of Access)

Does your child misbehave or act out when they are told no or when they are told they aren't allowed to have a particular snack or watch something on television? Sometimes that one word can set a child off if they don't know "the why" to the reason behind the word. If you need to deny access to your child, try using a word or phrase other than no; let them know why they can't do or have what they want; and then either offer an alternative or let them know when they can have what they want, whether it be the next day or another time you designate.

Sensory (Sensory Seeking)

Is your child getting their sensory needs met? Do they need to let out some frustration on a punching bag or pillow? Do they need squeezes from a stuffed animal? Maybe they are nervous and need to do some deep bubble or straw breathing. Whatever the case may be, if your child is a tactile stimulation or sensory seeking child, they might misbehave if their sensory needs aren't being met.

Communication (Lack of Speech and Language Skills)

Is your child able to talk yet? Maybe you have a young child with a speech or language delay or even a nonverbal child. Your child might have a difficult time expressing their needs verbally and thus get easily frustrated when they feel you don't know what they want or how to help. When a child can't effectively communicate to their caregiver, they often act out because of frustration, not because they want to be difficult.

How Do You Track Behavior?

The ABC chart is an evidence-based observation tool for behavior that was originally developed by psychologist Sidney Bijou in 1968. He proposed its use to analyze behavior patterns through A: Antecedents, B: Behavior, and C: Consequences. Antecedent is just a fancy term for what happens before an event. The best way to understand and modify a child's behavior and their motivation for misbehaving is by tracking it. A behavior chart will enable you to identify if the behavior is minor, moderate, or severe, as well as if there is a pattern. Tracking behavior will give you clues as to the child's motivation for misbehaving so you can find solutions.

Are they acting out at a particular time of day? Maybe it's midmorning because they are hungry and didn't have much of a breakfast, or maybe it's before bath time because they are tired and are going to bed too late. This is the time to unravel the rubber bands, get to the center of the Tootsie Pop, or unpeel all the onion layers to be your child's detective and identify patterns, actualize their behavior, and solve the case!

DATE	DAY	TIME	ANTECEDENT	BEHAVIOR	CONSEQUENCE	DURATION	SEVERITY
5/5/26	Tuesday	4:53PM	Said no to him when he wanted a toy	Heavy breathing, hitting, screaming, kicking, hyper-ventilating	Time out, denied access to TV/iPad	7 minutes	Mild, Moderate, or Severe

What Can You Do?

The best way to support a child who is misbehaving is to show them you care and provide them with the tools and skills to manage their actions. Your child is learning and won't always do things the "right" way or the best way. Give your child some grace for how they are behaving and teach them how you want them to act. Let them know the door is always open for them to talk to you. Even if they misbehaved or you don't agree with how they are feeling, validate them and let them know they are loved, respected, honored, seen, and heard. You can say, "I understand how you feel, and it's OK to feel that way. I have felt that way before, and it doesn't feel good. What can I do to help and support you?" Show them empathy and put yourself in your child's shoes. Let them know you understand how they feel despite how they acted.

Give a Task

When a child is misbehaving, one of the best ways to get them back on a positive behavior track is by making them feel special and useful. Children want to feel like they matter and that they are needed, especially if they are seeking connection. Do they need to feel important? Give them a task to be your helper. Give them purpose and a sense of power and control. Give them choices and help them feel empowered.

Connect and Play

Is your child feeling neglected because you have been busy? Do you need to reconnect? Take a few moments and play a short game with them or take them on a walk in the neighborhood. Play is typically always the best medicine and exactly what the doctor ordered.

Chapter 5

Positive Behavior Support Parenting

"Keep your thoughts positive because your thoughts become your words. Keep your words positive because your words become your behavior. Keep your behavior positive because your behavior becomes your habits."

—Mahatma Gandhi

A FEW YEARS BEFORE BECOMING A MOM, I WAS HIRED TO work as a program manager for a Positive Behavior Interventions and Supports (PBIS) program at a local nonprofit organization. I was in charge of supporting the implementation of a PBIS program in twenty elementary schools across multiple school districts. For years I led school-wide assemblies and trainings, and taught administrators, teachers, and staff how to focus on a child's positive behavior rather than their problematic behavior.

It's typical for parents to get stuck in a vortex pattern and mainly focus on a child's challenging behaviors. We can sometimes take for granted when our child is doing something right because it's common sense to us. For example, when a child sits in their chair at the table for mealtime, it's a clear expectation, so we don't make a big deal out of it when they do it. But we will certainly notice when our child is out of their chair during mealtime and even possibly reprimand them for it. The shift in perspective isn't hard, but not all parents buy into a positive behavioral support approach even though it's been proven effective by evidence-based research. If you are one of those skeptical parents, let me try to convince you otherwise.

What Is PBIS?

According to my PBIS mentor, Dr. Jeffrey Sprague, coauthor of Best Behavior: Building Positive Behavior Support in Schools, PBIS is a unique yet simple approach to problem behavior. At its core, PBIS provides effective strategies to support desired behaviors and improve behavior outcomes. The core principles of PBIS include developing clear expectations; clearly communicating and teaching appropriate behavioral actions; reinforcing positive behavior while minimizing attention to problem behavior; and having understandable, concise, and consistent consequences.

Parents often make the mistake of assuming their child knows how they are expected to behave or what it looks like to "be good." Parents often lack specificity when it comes to praising or correcting a child's behavior. When you say "be good" or "make sure you behave" to your child, do they know what you mean? Do they have a clear picture of what you expect of them? If not, they will most likely disappoint you and end up getting in trouble. When a parent is specific in their behavior requests, there is a smaller margin for error, which results in more positive behavior.

If a child feels like they are constantly getting in trouble by their parent, what's in it for them to behave? If they feel like being reprimanded is the only attention they are getting from their parent, their motivation is to misbehave. That doesn't mean parenting has to only be positive with no consequences. It's not all or nothing. There just has to be some thoughtful structure and balance. And if it can be heavier on the side of positive support rather than corrective criticism, you will be in a much different headspace and your child's behavior outcomes will look much different, which benefits both of you. In fact, PBIS gurus conclude that it takes a 4:1 ratio of reinforcing positive behavior to problematic behavior for optimal change. Research has shown that if a parent focuses on a child's positive behavior, the child will repeat this behavior time and time again. So why wouldn't you want to parent this way?

Intrinsic vs. Extrinsic Motivation

Two different types of motivation can help your child feel more empowered and engaged: intrinsic and extrinsic. These types of motivation can also provide children a greater sense of self-efficacy, self-competence, and self-confidence to get their homework done, help with chores around the house, and feel good about themselves.

INTRINSIC MOTIVATION	EXTRINSIC MOTIVATION
Intrinsic motivation comes from within, a sense of wanting to get something done because it feels good or because it's the right thing to do. Intrinsic motivation is very values based. Older children are more likely to conceptualize doing what's right without getting a reward or praise.	Extrinsic motivation is based on external validation and praise. Extrinsic motivation is often done via a reward system, such as a sticker chart, prize system, or monetary "token economy" program. Younger children tend to respond better to extrinsic motivation.

When I was implementing this program in schools, one of the concerns that kept coming up was about intrinsic versus extrinsic motivation. Why should children be rewarded for doing the right thing? Shouldn't children want to do the right thing out of the goodness of their heart? The short answer to those questions is yes. Children should want to do the right thing and they also need encouragement and incentives as well. It's not either/or, it is both/and. While intrinsic motivation derives from internal satisfaction, extrinsic motivation is rooted in validation from others. Both feel good to a child at different times. Both drive positive behavior.

Play is driven from intrinsic motivation, and Rogers and Sawyers (1988) confirm that "children are intrinsically motived to learn through play" (p. 114). Homework, chores, and other less-preferred tasks are typically extrinsically motivated. Children do these things because there is something in it for them, even if it's just because they want to avoid a consequence for not doing them. Very rarely will you find a young child initiate or jump at the chance to clean their room just because they like the aesthetics of a clean space and because it makes them feel good about themselves.

In a scholarly research article in *Contemporary Educational Psychology* titled "Intrinsic and Extrinsic Motivation from a Self-Determination Theory Perspective: Definitions, Theory, Practices, and Future Directions," Richard M. Ryan and Edward L. Deci write, "Competence concerns the feeling of mastery, a sense that one can succeed and grow. The need for competence is best satisfied within well-structured environments that afford optimal challenges, positive feedback, and opportunities for growth." When given positive reinforcement and upon completion of a task, children gain a sense of accomplishment and competence. They know internally they did something good, which in turn makes them feel good. This sense of goodness inspires them to continue doing good things for themselves and others, at first with external validation when they are young, then using internal validation as they get older.

But what happens when your child pre-negotiates their "reward" and tells you they will only do a particular task for a reward? In this case there is a power struggle. And that is why providing any type of reward should be done intermittently, when you catch them being good. You can still provide praise and positive feedback, but you don't always have to pair it with a reward. If your child asks, "What will I get if I do this?" you simply tell them they will get a high five or a hug or a verbal "good job" from you. If they argue with that, there is a deeper issue that needs to be resolved.

How to Implement a PBIS System in the Home

Evidence-based research shows that children want to comply, please their parents, and do the right thing. And teaching children behavioral expectations ahead of time will help them know the rules and want to repeat their positive behavior. When discussing the rules and behavior expectations for your home, focus on one behavior at a time. The first step is to set up rules for your home. These rules can be short and sweet like "be kind," "be safe," and "be accountable" or something along those lines. I wouldn't recommend having more than three to five rules for your home because children will have a difficult time retaining the information if there are too many or if they are too complicated. Once you have your rules, define them by creating a list of behavior expectations that go under each of the rules.

Then make your rules and expectations visual and colorful by

BE SAFE	BE KIND	BE ACCOUNTABLE
Use walking feet	Give compliments	Help with chores
Avoid playing on stairs	Use clean language	Do homework
Cross the street with an adult	Share toys	Make bed
Wear a helmet with bike	Say "please" and "thank you"	Brush teeth

adding fun clip art pictures next to the words for the younger children who cannot read. Hang these rules with the expectations on the fridge at your child's eye level.

Once you have the foundational components of your PBIS program, start implementing it by praising your child when they are behaving positively and complying with your expectations. This can be a verbal and or physical praise, a hug, or a high five, but be specific in your praise. Avoid saying, "You did a great job tonight at dinner." Instead say, "I loved how you sat still in your chair during dinner tonight!" Avoid saying, "Good job," but rather, "I am so proud of you for listening when I asked you to put your toys away." Your child will comprehend and internalize that you were happy with their behavior, and they will want to repeat that behavior. If they continue to forget the rules, instead of yelling at them or jumping to a consequence, calmly remind them of the behavior expectations. It's all about patience and repetition. This opportunity is a teaching moment and a way to improve your communication and connection with your child.

Daily or Weekly Behavior Report Cards

Some children are visual learners who also need tangible and consistent feedback. Pick one behavior your child needs to work on, such as sitting still in their chair at mealtime. Then create a chart that has breakfast, lunch, and dinner written on it with a box next to each one. If your child sits still at mealtime, give them a sticker for each meal, earning up to three stickers a day. This will help them visually and tangibly see their progress in small, digestible bites.

How to Implement a Two-Tiered Reinforcement System

Let's assume you want to maximize praise to achieve positive behavior. Some parents are skeptical of extrinsic validation, such as sticker charts, despite their effectiveness. I have used sticker charts in my home with my children and with my clients in private practice, and let me tell you, they work, and they work well! They are a helpful and powerful tool to teach children positive behavior. And don't worry, children won't depend on positive reinforcements forever. They will wean off them over time or once they achieve what they are working toward.

Incentives are effective, yet some parents believe they are bribing their child or rewarding them for behavior they should already be doing. These parents believe following behavior expectations should be motivated by intrinsic or internal validation. Eventually, most children will get to that sophisticated developmental level of behavior motivation, but when they are young, extrinsic motivation works better. If you find that your child isn't behaving positively or doing the things they are supposed to do and you are in a constant power struggle because of it, try giving positive praise and sticker charts a try.

Tier One

The first tier of reinforcement can be praise for smaller behaviors your child is doing positively. You can incentivize them with your positive attention, physical praise, and encouraging words. Children can be praised for doing more basic tasks, using kind language, positively regulating emotions, and following directions the first time they are asked. Parents can reinforce this behavior as much as they want.

Tier Two

The second tier of reinforcement can be for when your child goes above and beyond following the rules and behavior expectations. These reinforcements are saved for bigger-ticket items, like sleeping in their bed all night, helping with chores, not hitting or biting, or sharing toys with siblings or peers without protest. This is when a sticker might be given. Children can earn stickers to work toward a prize like time at the park, extra technology time, a later bedtime, an ice cream, or even a toy at the store.

One Last Note

Reinforcements should come as immediately as possible and be given with specificity. Intermittent reinforcements work best. When you give your child a positive reward, do not take that reward away if the child starts misbehaving. They earned that reward fair and square. If they misbehave, find another consequence to give them for that particular incident.

I'd also like to note that when you offer reinforcements to encourage positive behavior or when you give a consequence in response to a misbehaver, you aren't trying to emotionally control or irrationally manipulate your child by using threats or bribes for personal gain. Rather, setting a respectful and healthy boundary with your child protects your peace. When you calmly set limits, while giving your child autonomy to comply or not, you are respecting their choice and also providing positive praise if they cooperate and a natural consequence if they don't. You will learn more about this in future chapters.

Chapter 6

Solution-Focused Parenting

"We don't stop playing because we grow old. We grow old because we stop playing."

—George Bernard Shaw

FOR AS LONG AS I CAN REMEMBER, I HAVE BEEN TOLD THAT I am a positive person. Even in the worst of times I have been known for having an optimistic viewpoint and an ability to see the good in any situation. I have told myself that what has been done is in the past; therefore, I focus on what I can control in the present and future.

The way I conceptualize life, relationships, and clinical work is solution-focused. This theoretic orientation is based on my philosophy of life, which is grounded in solution-focused brief therapy (SFBT). As a parent, I also view behavior modification through a solution-focused lens. I try to focus on the solution, not the problem. I stay in the present, not the past. And I capitalize on a child's natural ability to rely on their coping skills, strengths, and positive outcomes.

That being said, SFBT, PBIS, and Play Therapy are all interconnected and complement each other extremely well. These evidence-based models are the trifecta of how to effectively parent to enhance connection, improve communication, and modify behavior. According to Nims (2007), "SFBT is relevant for working with young children. Expressive play therapy techniques are effective in facilitating this process." Furthermore, the foundation of SFBT includes several elements that are designed to elicit positive behaviors. Berg and Steiner (2003) also concluded that children's nonverbal, playful, and creative habits support successful therapy based on the SFBT model.

The History of Solution-Focused Therapy

Insoo Kim Berg and Steve de Shazer developed SFBT with their colleagues at the Brief Family Therapy Center in Milwaukee during the 1980s. The early work of Milton Erickson, known for brief and creative systemic theory-based family interventions, was also rooted in SFBT. SFBT is unique in that the theory incorporates relational collaboration, much like a parent and child relationship. Therefore, families collaborate on constructing solutions together.

According to Lee and Mjelde-Mossey (2004), a "fundamental assumption of solution-focused therapy is that all people, regardless of their level of functioning, have strengths, resources, and competencies." The emphasis of SFBT is underlined in the construction of finding a solution rather than solving the problem.

Another core principle of SFBT is that families are not bound to what has happened in the past; rather, they are focused on the present and the future. Because SFBT theorists believe that the future of a family is created and negotiated, even if a family suffered from dysfunction in the past, the family could make choices about the present that will lead to a functional future.

A solution-focused therapist encourages families to not repeat the same mistake; instead, they suggest that the family does something different if a problem persists. Doing something different can be challenging and requires creative thinking. In fact, the solution doesn't have to be directly related to the problem. If a rational solution was tried and tried again yet the problem still exists, an out-of-the-box idea may be what the family needs. These tenets align effortlessly with a play-based parenting approach.

How to Be a Solution-Focused Parent

When using a systemic perspective, the family consists of the parent and the child simultaneously. Both the parent and the child respond and react to each other's emotions and behaviors. One does not exist without the other. If a child is acting out behaviorally, the child isn't solely to blame for the problems within the household. Many times, when the parent reacts and responds differently to their child, the child's behavior also changes.

SFBT is a valuable therapy to use with children because children solve problems using trial and error. Children often do not know what caused a problem, and the origin of the problem usually doesn't matter. They are interested in what will work to solve the problem. Being experimental and creative is a child's way of expressing themselves and creating solutions. The greatest transformation comes from when the parent and child work together to cultivate change.

SFBT uses a variety of techniques to help families experience positive behaviors or solutions that determine the groundwork for new thinking. Let's start by creating a road map.

Creating a Road Map

A road map is a major SFBT component that will help families reach a solution quickly and successfully. To create a road map within the family, a solution-minded parent focuses on moving in a forward direction. Families can do this by making goals, including what desired behaviors they want to achieve in their home. Goals have to be concrete, positive-minded, behavioral, relevant, meaningful, and specific to the family's situation. "The more concrete and measurable the goal, the more potential there is for making progress toward solutions" (De Jong & Berg, 2002).

Parents can observe compliance between family members, how they behave with their child, how their child behaves with them, and what roles each parent takes in the relationship with the child. It is the theoretical belief of SFBT that the family is the expert on what needs to change. Honoring equally valid perspectives from both parent and child provides an opportunity for collaboration. Parents can compliment positive aspects and changes within the family system, as well as praise and encourage each other and what is working.

Similar to the evidence-based research done from a PBIS perspective, Mills and Sprenkle (1995) contend that language is the medium of change in SFBT. Communicating about solutions helps families conceptualize new thoughts that will promote change, and it is the goal of SFBT to "conduct conversations that are most useful for the client in getting results within a brief period of time" (Berg & Szabó, 2005). Sounds like when we parent in a crunch and need solutions quickly!

It's important to remember that inflections, tone of voice, and level of emotional intensity contribute to the meaning of a conversation. The family member speaking and the family member listening have an equal amount of responsibility in any given conversation. Although SFBT is a language-based therapy, it is important to remember that family members connect with more than the spoken word. They also communicate through body movements, nonverbal communication, and silence.

Also similar to a PBIS perspective, an underlying assumption of SFBT is that change is constant and inevitable. Change can be subtle, and it is important for a family to recognize positive change. Look for all the parenting wins, big and small!

Families can also assume that even the smallest solution can lead to a larger change. This coincides with "catching a child being good" and focusing on their positive behavior rather than their problematic behavior. The belief is that all systems can change. If the parent does not believe change can take place, the change process is inhibited. When parents are optimistic and highly motivated to solve an identified problem, they see themselves as part of the problem and an active participant in the change process. This mentality will cultivate longer-lasting and more effective changes within the family system and with their child.

A major characteristic of SFBT is moving a child toward new perspectives and behaviors via experimentation, much like a play-based parenting approach. In many ways, parenting is all about experimenting. It's about learning what works and what doesn't work with your child. Each child is different, and there is no cookie-cutter way to raise a child, although I still have to argue that positive, solution-focused, play-based strategies are more effective than other traditional parenting methods. Thus, I believe that experimentation is a key element of parenting. Experimentation often requires a parent to think outside the box for a more positive, solution-focused, and playful solution. According to Berg and Szabó (2005), "calling it an experiment indicates that it is not a cure that coaches will prescribe to students but implies playfulness" (p. 98). In SFBT, parents focus primarily on:

- What they are doing that's working
- What the desired change is
- What resources the family has
- How motivated they are
- How the family works together on finding solutions

- How they cope through challenging moments
- What the family has done that has worked in the past
- What the family has not done that they are willing to try

Families should adopt both/and thinking toward possible options, and as previously mentioned, families should theoretically believe that change is possible and there is hope for positive outcomes in a brief amount of time.

From an SFBT lens, each family member is to have a voice and share thoughts and solutions. They also regularly cultivate:

- Encouragement
- Empowerment
- Hope
- Optimism
- Positivity
- Confidence
- Compliments

Solution-Focused Parenting Techniques and Interventions

How can a parent shift their mindset to focus on the solution and not the problem? Let's say your child bites their sibling.

- First, the parent sets a limit and tells the child that biting is not acceptable or safe. This helps pause the problematic behavior and explains *why* that behavior wasn't OK. It also focuses on the behavior rather than the emotion that provoked it.
- Then the parent redirects the child to bite down on a toy teether to get the same sensory effect they're desiring, or, if

they're a little older, to hit a punching bag or pillow, stomp their feet, or yell "I'm mad at you!" rather than bite their sibling.

The solution lies not just in the replacement behavior but in the teaching moment and the repetition of the parent's behavior expectations.

FOCUSING ON THE PROBLEM	FOCUSING ON THE SOLUTION
"It's so frustrating. You always bite your sister. You never listen when I tell you to stop. I don't know what to do anymore." In this scenario, the focus is on the child's negative behavior and the frequency and intensity of the problem. The emphasis is on what is *not* working, helplessness, and hopelessness.	"Let's figure out how to stop this behavior together." Take inventory of the situation. What mood am I in? What is motivating my child's behavior? Think of what the child responds well to and what they are doing when they aren't biting. The emphasis is on what *is* working, exceptions, strengths, and possibilities for change—instilling a sense of agency and hope.

Solution-focused parenting frees you from automatically punishing your child for every errant behavior and instead empowers you to support them in identifying what they require and addressing the need for a different behavioral outcome in a safe and positive way.

Franklin et al. (2001) contend it's vital to "amplify positive behaviors and reinforce the use of effective coping strategies" (p. 411). De Shazer (1991) promotes solution talk and change talk as important elements of the theory. One therapeutic technique is asking questions starting with simple words like perhaps, instead, suppose, and what else. These words are considered tentative language. Tentative language is a conversation strategy that allows a solution-focused therapist to offer possibilities to families without offending the family members. This technique encourages the family to conceptualize an ideal situation by collaborating and using creative thinking skills. A family's imagination is a key component in turning a problem into a solution. Dwelling too long on the problem can lengthen the process and prolong attempts to find solutions so change can take place.

The Miracle Question

One of the most recognized techniques of SFBT is "the miracle question." The miracle question helps families visualize, clarify, and reach goals by imagining that the problem they are experiencing has disappeared overnight. They are also asked what others might notice about their problem if it changed. This empowers them to construct change.

To make it more play-based, ask a child what would change if there was a magic wand, fairy dust, or toy that could change something in their life. They can also draw it, act it out, or play it out in a sand tray. A child could also be asked what their life would look like if it were more playful and connected, or what it would look like if they behaved better. Adapting it for a parent asking a child, it could look like this: "If there was something we could work on together that would help you feel different, what would that be?" (Nims, 2007).

Scaling

Another foundational technique that solution-focused therapists use is scaling. Solution-focused therapists will ask family members to rate something on a scale from one to ten. Typically, one means the problem is debilitating and ten means the problem no longer exits. Children respond well to using numbers rather than words, and scaling helps them shift perspectives from a negative one to a positive one with regard to making a change.

A parent can ask a child to rate their behavior on a scale from one to ten. A one means the behavior is at its worst and a ten means the behavior is at its best. Then, depending on their number, ask how the child will reach a higher number. If a child reports behavior being at a four, ask, "What do you have to do to be a six? What does a six look like?"

A parent can also ask a child what is better, the same, or worse. If something is better from day to day or week to week, the family then thinks about what was done differently so they can repeat the pattern. If something is the same, it is actually seen as a positive because it is not worse, and the family concludes they have been functioning at the same level as they were previously. If a behavior worsened, they could intervene appropriately.

Exceptions to Behaviors

Another fundamental technique of SFBT is asking exception questions. These types of questions are considered simple tools to help families recognize when the problem doesn't exist. Many times, parents will notice when a child is misbehaving and focus on negative behaviors. Exploring when a child is doing what they are supposed to be doing is finding exceptions to when the child is doing something that needs correction. When has your child not acted out this week? When did they behave? A problem does not persist in every situation. A solution-focused parent can ask if there is an exception to the problem and what it might look like if the problem didn't exist in the future. Identifying the exception—the period of time when the problem does not exist or is diminished—helps parents conceptualize change. By finding exceptions to problems, they seem less overwhelming. Exceptions also encourage parents to be fluid and not fixed.

Identifying Coping Skills

Coping questions are also imperative techniques of SFBT. Coping questions focus on asking how parents have managed to cope so far with the current situation that the family desires to change. A solution-focused therapist might ask parents what keeps them going through difficult times. Coping questions are asked when parents appear to be overwhelmed or hopeless. Answers to these questions often lead parents to find a small accomplishment in what they are already doing. It's important to remember that small wins are still wins. A coping skill might mean reaching out and asking for support and help. It may also mean leaning on another caregiver, neighbor, or friend to give you a break. So next time you are feeling overwhelmed with parenting your bundles of joy, go back to your coping toolbox and do what works to help you move forward.

Do you think you have what it takes to be a solution-focused-minded parent?

PART II

Manifesting Intentional Play-Based Parenting

Chapter 7

Prioritizing Playdates, a YES Attitude, and Putting Your Media Away to Play

"Children don't say, 'I had a bad day, can we talk?' They say, 'Will you play with me?'"

—Lawrence Cohen

WHEN I HAVE CLIENTS SHARE WITH ME THAT THEIR CHILD IS "acting up" or is jealous of another sibling (this happens especially for toddlers with a new baby), one of the first things I ask is how much dedicated playtime the parent is spending with their child each week. If the parent tells me they aren't spending any one-on-one time with their child, I recommend they start regularly scheduling one-on-one dedicated playdates, or what I like to call "purposeful play pockets."

In other words, I suggest that each parent intentionally carve out space on their calendar for undivided time with their child to engage in a play-focused activity. Going to the grocery store or post office together doesn't count. Sometimes, giving much-needed attention and providing a special connection with a child are all they need to start behaving better. It sounds simple, but it's true. If a child feels loved and secure with their parents, their behavior starts heading in a positive direction. Playdates don't have to cost a lot of money or even take a lot of time. The only rules are to be present, play together in some way, and have no technology distractions.

There are so many benefits to having dedicated playtime with your children. Spending time with each child is important for their self-worth, self-image, and overall emotional, mental, and social well-being. Dedicated playtime will also:

- Enhance your relationship with your child
- Create a stronger and healthier secure attachment
- Lessen negative attention-seeking behavior
- Lessen temper tantrums
- Create long-lasting, positive memories
- Teach your child relationship and communication skills
- Teach your child the importance of family values
- Strengthen parent-child communication

Purposeful Play Pockets

Whether you call it dedicated time, dating your children, scheduled family playdates, or a purposeful play pocket of time, spending one-on-one time with your child (whether you have one child or several) makes a huge difference in their behavior. All children need dedicated alone time with their parent(s) to openly discuss anything on their mind or just to release and have fun in a safe and sacred environment.

Make sure to put the playdate on the calendar in advance (or something else will come up or you'll forget). As parents, we have good intentions but tend to get busy, and if it's not planned ahead, it may not happen. I know we have a lot on our plates, but trust me, this extra effort pays off. Children, especially the older ones, will hold you accountable for this time. It is something they look forward to and depend on, so be consistent and follow through. Children will see the playdate on the calendar and look forward to it, increasing their positive behavior because they know they will have special time with you and your undivided attention.

Daily playdates can be going to get the mail together each afternoon or making a meal together, playing a board game, or taking a walk together in the neighborhood. These are quick and simple yet effective.

If you have more than one child, this process is even more important, as each child needs dedicated time with each parent, without their sibling/s. Siblings can trade off weeks if need be or, if you have two children, one parent can take out one child while the other parent takes out the other.

I also recommend a date outside the home once a week or once a month, depending on the age of your child, how persistent their behavior is, and how much they need you. I recommend checking ahead of time to see what events are taking place in or around your city for that month. Set the date and time as well as childcare for siblings if needed. Maybe there is a special event, festival, or museum exhibit coming to town that you can attend. You may need to make reservations or buy tickets in advance, so plan ahead. The most important part is to follow through. Life happens, people get sick, and things come up, but these playdates should be a priority. If you have to cancel, set a new date as quickly as possible.

As they get older, your children will also have ideas about what they want to do during your special playdates, so I suggest empowering them and letting them be involved with the process. Have them come up with a wish list of what they would like to do with you, and you can pick from that list based on your time and budget that month.

As a mom of two, I know how busy life can get. It's easy to get stuck in the daily grind and day-to-day routines. We all have things we need to do, but not everything is urgent. Decide what you can put off until tomorrow and go play with your child. Role-model what it looks like to block out your calendar, make time for yourself, and prioritize play.

If I haven't said it enough yet throughout this book, play is a priority. It not only helps connection with your child, it will also help modify their behavior. Setting aside time to take your child to play at the park or pick out some new books at the library for an hour once a week will be very special for them, and you'll both reap the benefits.

These dates should not necessarily be a reward for good behavior or taken away because of negative behavior. They should be treated as a necessity to your relationship and a component to your daily, weekly, or monthly routine. If you take this special playdate away as a punishment because of bad behavior, their behavior may get worse. If you reward your child with a playdate for good behavior, they will feel like they have to earn your love, which can also have negative outcomes. Your child needs connection to you, no matter how they behave. If they misbehave the morning of your scheduled playdate, provide an appropriate consequence related to the misbehavior but proceed on your playdate as planned. Use this time to reconnect and reset.

Playdates should be spent screen-free with active participation, active listening, and active involvement with your child. Be intentional and avoid scrolling social media, constantly texting, or having your child spend a lot of time on their tablet while you're together. If you want to take some photos on your phone to remember your time together, keep it brief and make sure that's all you do. Resist the urge to reply to a notification or become disengaged from your child.

The reason this playdate recipe works so well is because of three ingredients: connection, play, and intentionality. When a child feels seen, heard, and valued, they feel safe and connected, which ultimately leads to better behavior. When they feel loved, they are happy and will want to make you happy.

Put Your Media Away and Play

I remember a family session I had many years ago with a parent and their child. The child was expressing that their parent wasn't spending time with them and how it felt. The parent became defensive and responded that they did spend time with their child. The child then responded, "You sit on the couch next to me while I am watching a show, but you're on your phone the entire time." I will never forget that moment or that conversation. The parent probably thought they were legitimately spending time with their child, but the child knew the parent wasn't present with them at all. There was no eye contact, no back-and-forth conversation, not even a moment to discuss the show they could have been watching together. The child sat next to their parent night after night in this scenario and felt ignored and isolated.

Active vs. Passive Participation

The way I see it, there are two different types of parental participation:

ACTIVE PARTICIPATION	PASSIVE PARTICIPATION
Active participation means the parent is intentionally involved, present, and participating at an engaging level. There is eye contact and reciprocal communication. Talking, playing a board game, bike riding together, or cooking in the kitchen are some ways parents can actively participate with their children.	*Passive participation* means the parent is physically in the same room but is not present or engaged. The parent or child is on a device, or they are both mindlessly on the couch, watching a show together, but there is no shared commentary, laughter, or thoughts discussed during or after the show.

Although it seems impossible, I will be sharing helpful strategies on how to be intentional, present, and actively engaged with your children. We live in a technological world, and screen time is a dominant and active part of our culture. It can even be considered intrusive. Media also takes us away from the present moment, pulls our attention away from what is right in front of us, and minimizes the value of playing. Learning mindfulness strategies helps parents focus on being playful with their children without the distraction of a television, tablet, or phone. I have noticed in my practice and with my own children that the more I am distracted, the worse my children's behavior becomes. If I am present and intentional without technological distractions, my children behave better. Connection and behavior go hand in hand, and this chapter will help parents achieve a new, mindful way to interact with their children to attain more positive behavior.

We are currently living in a technology-driven era. As parents, we are challenged to find the right balance of screen time and media use for our modern family, and it's not an easy task. I didn't grow up with a cell phone, but now I am raising children who are born into a digitally driven world and are exposed to media devices at birth. Media consumption is the cause of many power struggles and meltdowns between parents and children, causing more disruptive behavior. You can achieve more positive behavior by reducing technological distractions, and this chapter will show you how.

Media devices can be a tool for education and entertainment; however, they have become a source of addiction for parents and children. Excessive media use is affecting our mental health by causing anxiety and depression as well as lower attention spans. Screen consumption provides instant gratification and fast-paced communication at our fingertips. Each time we get notified of a new text message or a new like on our social media posts, we get a dopamine rush. And that's difficult for a parent to compete with. *Media use creates a dopamine release in our brains that can cause a chemical reac-*

tion similar to drugs, so it's easy to have withdrawal symptoms when you detox from it.

For parents, media is our lifeline. And it is challenging to live without it. However, without boundaries, extreme screen use can lead to altered mood and behavioral issues, hindered sleep, classroom or work performance issues, and increased mental health challenges. And unmonitored screen time for children can also lead to an increase in cyberbullying, pornography viewing, erratic and disruptive behavior, and exposure to traumatic content that is not age appropriate.

Pediatricians recommend the following guidelines for children's screen time:

UNDER TWO YEARS OLD	TWO TO FIVE YEARS OLD	FIVE TO SEVENTEEN YEARS OLD
No screen time except for occasional video chatting	No more than one hour per day of co-viewing with a parent	No more than two hours per day except for homework

But here's the problem with the "except for homework" rule. Some children are getting iPads provided by school districts as early as Pre-K. They do a lot of "work" on them during the day at school and then are expected to use them at home to do homework, which can easily take up that two-hour recommendation.

So what do we do? My first recommendation would be to silence your devices and turn off notifications to lessen urgency and time online. I would also set some time limits and boundaries for when and how you use your device. There are social and entertainment benefits to using media devices, but due to its addictive nature, it's difficult to control ourselves.

I think the sooner a parent can set a precedent around media use in the home, the better. Set the expectation level as soon as possible and enforce it often. Boundaries and limits can be set around how much time is used per day or if it is used between certain hours or at the dinner table. I believe parents need to follow the same rules as their children. If a parent doesn't want their child on their media device during mealtime, then the parent shouldn't be on their media device during that time, either.

If a parent wants to help their child feel like they have special privileges the older they become, they can increase the time limits at home by fifteen minutes at each birthday. Start low so there is room to grow each year. This way the older siblings feel a little more special than their younger siblings, at least in the area of media use.

Normalize being off media and make it a part of your family's culture. Put value on spending time focusing on being outside, playing, body movement, and participating in other activities that do not require a screen. And instead of regularly allowing screen time or taking screen time away as a punishment, spin it into a positive by letting the child earn technology time for completing homework, doing chores, spending time playing outside, or doing acts of kindness. They can earn time minute for minute, so if your child does twenty-three minutes of chores, they earn twenty-three minutes of screen time. Or you can arrange a flat time, and after A, B, and C are done, they can get an automatic twenty minutes of screen time. This way the child controls whether they earn screen time, or extra screen time, that day.

Once you've set a precedent in your home and have established limits and boundaries around media use, practice on being intentional, mindful, playful, and present. Does your child get off a screen and transition to a non-screen activity quickly and without protest? What about you? Let's do a media detox experiment. See how your mental health and how present you are change after one week of limited media use. Then see how your child's mood and behavior change after one week.

Take the time you would typically scroll social media, watch a show on television, or keep your child busy with a tablet, and replace it with taking a walk outside, playing in the backyard, going to the park, playing board games, or doing a craft. I encourage you to take notes throughout the week and possibly even brain dump or journal your thoughts and observations each day.

The first day might be difficult, and you may feel yourself going through emotional, mental, and even physical withdrawal symptoms. You may even feel desperate and try to convince yourself that you can't do it. Your child might have a few tantrums when you tell them they can't watch their favorite show on television or play their favorite game on their tablet. But despite the challenges, I encourage you to keep going. I predict that by the third or fourth day, you won't miss your media time, and neither will your child. It might take a little more effort on your part, but observe if your relationship with your child improves or feels closer; see if your child's behavior is more positive; evaluate your own mood and energy level; and notice whether you are more present throughout the day. I can almost guarantee that your life will dramatically change for the better when you put your media away and play.

Cultivating a YES Attitude

I came up with the YES Attitude with my own children a few years ago and now consider it my own personal philosophy. I caught myself saying no to my children more times than I was saying yes. For me, it was how I had a sense of control. I would habitually say no to my children because doing whatever they were asking wasn't on my agenda for the day, or I was too tired to participate or help with them with a particular project. I quickly realized I had to put myself in check and flip my mindset around to have a more welcoming and positive attitude toward my children's requests. That meant that if they asked to paint, instead of me thinking it would make too much of a mess that I didn't want to clean up, I needed to put their play needs before my own and let them paint and make a mess—with some healthy limits and guidelines of course. To a parent, the child's work is a mess; to a child, it's their masterpiece.

I also noticed a shift in behavior with my clients over the years when their parents started saying yes to requests more than they said no. I have asked parents to keep a tally chart on their fridge and track all the times they said yes and all the times they said no to their child. They are typically surprised by how often they are saying no and are frequently shocked by the fact that they are saying no more than yes.

When a child repeatedly hears the word no, a few things generally happen: They will stop asking, secretly become resentful toward their parent, and detach emotionally around them; or they will become resentful and act out more because they will do what they want to do anyway. Defiance and deception start taking center stage, and parents are left wondering why their child is misbehaving. Behavior is usually interconnected within a system—it doesn't typically just show up out of the blue or because the child was born that way. Yes, there are some neurological differences in the brain that some children may have, or some personality and temperament traits that may add fuel to the fire, but there is always a reason a child is acting out. Sometimes, it's honestly just in how they are parented and how the parent and child react and respond to one another.

This isn't to say that a parent has to say yes to their child all the time, because trust me, that leads to entitlement. But there needs to be a balance—the ratio needs to be more positive than negative. Even if it's just 2:1, make sure you're saying yes more than you're saying no. Find a way to make it work, for your child's sake. Trust me, you will all come out happier in the end.

Saying yes to a mess is temporary, but the lasting effects on your child's well-being will skyrocket to a whole new level. Next time you want to say no as an impulse, pause and ask yourself, "Why not?" Ask yourself what's the worst that could happen if you say yes.

Remember, you aren't saying yes every time they ask. You still have boundaries and limits, but in that fleeing moment, what is the worst that could happen? Could you say yes in that moment? A YES Attitude will ultimately help your children behave more positively.

If your child asks to paint your walls with finger paint, that would be a hard no. If they ask to eat an entire cake, that too would be an emphatic no. We are talking extremes here, but I also recognize that children love to push buttons and boundaries with their parents to see what they can get away with. That being said, compromise and negotiate with them instead of automatically turning them down. Instead, tell them they can paint on the backyard fence with washable paint or color with chalk on the garage door. Sometimes children just want to do something they perceive as pushing a limit without actually being destructive.

When your child asks for something, first respond with "why?" Ask them to explain their rationale. If they are on the younger side, they might just say "because I want to" or "I don't know," but challenge them a little and try to get them to think about why that cookie is important or why doing a particular activity means so much to them. How will this enhance their life?

If you say no automatically without hearing them out, a power struggle or tantrum is inevitable. Put the ball back in their court and give them the floor. They might just surprise you and have a really good reason why this particular request is important to them. This also leaves room to negotiate and compromise. Maybe you won't be able to give them the moon, but you can give them a sliver of it.

Plus, when you say yes when they least expect you to, you become the hero. It might only last until the next request comes along, but the impression will be long-lasting. And then when you actually have to say no for a good reason, you have some padding to fall back on. You can remind them of all the times you said yes, so they know you will likely say yes again, just not this particular time.

I know there are parents out there who are uncomfortable with messes and can be obsessive about cleanliness and order. When we say no and deny our children the freedom and opportunity to play and make messes (without cleaning up their creations immediately) it hinders their creativity and belief they are safe to express themselves. Saying no in this case is more about our own anxiety and need for power and control. If a parent says no because they have a need for control, that is a more difficult habit to break. If a parent says no due to their anxiety, they will have an easier time shifting to a YES Attitude. They may be anxious that their child will make too much of a mess, get physically or emotionally hurt by taking a healthy risk, or eat too much sugar and get sick, and those are all totally valid concerns. Those are typically the reasons I say no a lot, too. I am my child's protector and as a grown adult with a fully developed brain, I logically know what's best for my child.

But children are told what to do almost every single day of their lives by an adult, whether it's a parent, a teacher, or a coach. Children normally don't call the shots, but what if they could, if only for a moment? When is the last time you viewed the world through a child's eyes? Have you forgotten what it's like to think and act like a child? Children hang on to yes moments like gold. A little yes goes a long way!

And if you can do more than a yes moment, how about an entire YES Day? I call these "ultimate play days." It's basically a day dedicated to the child, where they choose the activities for the day, within reason, and the parent is to say yes all day. Don't panic, there are limits. There are financial limits, physical limits, and yes, even eating limits. Don't worry, your child won't be eating ice cream and doughnuts all day or spending thousands of dollars visiting a theme park and buying everything in sight.

Let me ask you this: What is the harm in saying yes? What is holding you back? What is making you feel like you have to say no? What if your child had some control for a day? Would you allow that? It might just change the dynamics of your relationship with your child and their behavior.

I was recently talking about YES Days with a few moms after school, and they were both adamant that they would never let their children have one. One mom looked visibly anxious just thinking about it, and I kept wondering, why not? I know her children would love it. In fact, she said they had asked for one on multiple occasions. The other mom likes order and control. She said she didn't trust her children to pick anything she would actually say yes to—but that was just her assumption. I can understand on a psychological level why a YES Day made them so uncomfortable, but instead of having compassion for these moms, I could feel myself getting angry about it. And here's why: Their rigidness was a detriment to their child because they only saw things from their anxiety-ridden, controlling perspective. A YES Day made them uncomfortable, but was that really what their children needed?

When you parent out of anxiety or fear of not having control, it has negative ramifications on the child. Studies have shown that anxiety is passed down generationally, so if the parent is anxious, the child has a higher risk of being anxious, too. In fact, a 2019 review analyzed twenty-five studies that all concluded that children were significantly more likely to have anxiety and depressive disorders if their parent had an existing anxiety disorder. The worst part about all of this is that many parents with anxiety don't see it within themselves. If you bring it up, these parents get defensive and deny their anxiety. Therefore, they don't change their behavior, and their children are susceptible to anxious tendencies.

These children run the risk of having more generalized anxiety, separation anxiety, social anxiety, and specific phobias. They don't acclimate to school or social situations well and have irrational fears as well as a harder time adjusting to new environments, separating from their parent, and sleeping through the night. They may even have trouble eating a variety of food, traveling, or venturing out of their comfort zone. These children also run the risk of frequent meltdowns and or panic attacks.

Before you can become a YES parent and have a YES Attitude, ask yourself what you are anxious about and why you need to have control. Then figure out ways to manage those needs. What are your biggest fears? What is the worst-case scenario? What are you so worried will happen? Once you are able to come to honest terms with yourself and your own state of mind, you will be free to be a YES parent! It's worth the work and the effort. You will feel better about your parenting style, and your children will benefit from it. But how do you get there?

As much of this book preaches, this type of parenting is a mindset change, a shift in perspective. It might be a little challenging at first if this isn't your typical parenting style, but with some practice it will become more natural. You will have to retrain your brain and not act on familiarity and impulse because innately you'll want to say no. Your brain just goes there. It might be different from how you were raised, and it's difficult to change intergenerational parenting patterns. But this way of parenting is important and life-changing. And if you start parenting this way when your children are young, you will have a deeper, more trusting relationship with them, which will help you tremendously when they are older, especially in those challenging teenage years!

Chapter 8

Less Overparenting, More Autonomy

"When you're free, you can play. And when you are playing, you become free."

—Heidi Kadison

THIS CHAPTER WILL HELP PARENTS IDENTIFY IF THEY ARE overparenting their children, discuss the dangers of overparenting, and give practical ways parents can give their child more authority and autonomy. It will also provide reasons why unstructured and unsupervised play is important to developmental growth. Parents will learn the benefits of independent play and performing skills and activities solo. There are so many parents who want to be in the same room with their children while they play, or who set up a structured play activity that requires the parent to be present and help every step of the way. Although there is a time and place for activities like these, children won't learn the benefits of play or use their own imagination and creativity if a parent is constantly present and involved. This chapter will help parents let go and allow the protected space for their children to play outside in the backyard without a parent watching and commenting on their every move. And instead of a parent coming up with the play idea, the child is given the power and autonomy to choose their own play activity—especially one that doesn't require a parent's assistance.

I can't tell you how many times this subject comes up for me professionally. I have been on the news more times than I can count to talk about the dangers of being a coddling parent. I first discussed this topic on FOX 5 San Diego, and then I made my national news debut on Dr. Phil's *The News on Merit Street* on the Merit Street Media network.

I define a coddling parent as a parent who overprotects, over-shields, over-consoles, and overwhelms their children. These parents have a hard time letting go and handling their child's emotions because they also have trouble regulating themselves. Coddling parents tend to come from a place of anxiety, fear, and a need for control. These types of parents also try to hold their child responsible for their own emotions and behaviors. They are enmeshed with their child at an unhealthy level but are also defensive and in denial about it.

A coddling parent tends to answer questions for their children, steps in to solve all of a child's problems (ones that a child is fully capable of handling on their own), and overprotects them from any failure or uncomfortable emotion that comes their way. It also means they over-console their child if they get emotionally or physically hurt. A coddling parent does not allow their child to make their own decisions, does not allow them to experience failure or wrongdoing, and is extremely needy and controlling. They tend to be everywhere their child is and are only far enough away to swoop in quickly if they perceive their help is needed. They will go to extremes to not let their children suffer or fail, like doing their homework or calling their teachers or friend's parents on their behalf if there is an issue.

I believe these parents get a bad rap, and these labels can be somewhat damaging to parents who love their children and are doing the best they can; however, there is a more effective way to parent children without coddling them. Being an "involved" parent can have its benefits, and if the engagement is kept at an appropriate level, this type of parent can develop a deep bond with their child. With this close, secure bond, they can also have preventive and proactive conversations about risk factors, social matters at school, and awareness of issues with peers, teachers, and grades. This is beneficial if there is a problem beyond your child's control, so you can support them if needed. If it goes beyond that, then pause and reconsider how "involved" you actually are and if you are hindering your child's autonomy. There is a big difference between offering advice to help your child overcome an obstacle and handling the situation for them.

If a parent is showing empathy and validation in a gentle way, they are in tune with their child and can more easily help them when a problem arises. Coddling parents mean well and want to "protect" their child, so their parenting method comes from a good, caring place. They just don't want to see their child hurt, but so much so that they go to the extreme, assuming their child isn't able to cope with anything problematic. *When the going gets tough, show your child it's OK to sit in the mess, then give them guidance on how to get up again.*

Teaching a Growth Mindset

Instead of being a coddling parent, try to be a growth mindset parent. A growth mindset is a philosophy about how to view life through a positive and fluid lens. Having a growth mindset is more about the process than the outcome—it's about the effort and the attitude of a task. With a growth mindset, a child's challenge, mistake, or even a failed attempt at something isn't looked at as the end or an excuse to give up. Rather, it helps a child embrace the temporary setback and gives them a reason to try harder or from a different angle the next time.

The ultimate goal is to encourage your child to make small but steady steps toward goals and empower them to handle challenging life situations. Have you ever heard your child say "I'm not good enough" or "I'm stupid" or "I can't do it"? It's pretty common with children. But teaching them to have a growth mindset creates a love for learning, a greater strength to try new and difficult things, and a sense of resilience when obstacles come their way. Let me ask you this: Is a winner someone who never loses or someone who gets up after getting knocked down?

Examples of a Growth Mindset vs. a Fixed Mindset

FIXED MINDSET	GROWTH MINDSET
A child says, "I can't do it."	A parent says, "I know it's difficult, but you just haven't figured it out yet."
A child says, "I am stupid."	A parent says, "You made a mistake on that math problem, but you can fix it the next time."
A child says, "I did it, but . . ."	A parent says, "You did it, and . . ."
A child says, "I'm not good enough."	A parent says, "I know you are disappointed. Let's take a break and try again tomorrow."
A child says, "I'm not going to try because I don't want to fail."	A parent says, "You will only fail when you stop trying."
A child says, "I will read two books this week."	A parent says, "I love your passion for reading. Let's read more tomorrow than we did yesterday and see how many books we can read by the end of the week."

A child says, "I want to get all A's this year."	A parent says, "That is a great goal. I want you to try your best and enjoy what you learn."
A child says, "I am not good at . . ."	A parent says, "It will get easier when you practice! And if not, let's try something else you are good at!"

If a child asks their coddling parent to "back off," the parent usually feels betrayed. A parent may respond, "How dare you, after everything I've done for you." It is difficult to prove to a coddling parent that their child is capable. And when they do allow their child to do something on their own, they are the first to see them fail and say, "I told you so." A coddling parent needs to feel needed and in control. A child can try to gain more autonomy as they get older, but there will be a power struggle. It might be best for those children to try to find autonomy in places other than home.

Be active in your child's life, but don't control it. Children need to fail just as much as they need to succeed—they need to fall and then learn how to get back up. Overparenting is more about a parent's anxiety than it is about effective parenting. The next time you go to clean their dishes or do their laundry, pause and then teach them how to do these tasks. They may not do them correctly, quickly, or the way you would do them, but let them learn their own way.

This non-anxious parenting should also take place when your child is learning a new skill, playing, doing homework, or making a project. Although it might be tempting, try not to help them as much as you'd like to (in other words, don't do their work for them), and try not to correct the moves they make if it's not "perfect" or the way you think it should be done. Give them the freedom to try it on their own. And if they ask for help, ask, "How do you think it should be done?" Help them be critical thinkers and problem solvers by putting the ball back in their court. This also means coming to terms with the fact that your children aren't fragile.

It's important to provide your child the opportunity to develop healthy risks. Let them get dirty outside. Don't worry, they can take a bath and wash their clothes. This might heighten your anxiety, but don't let that get in the way of your child's development. Let them jump off the slide and scrape their knee. A bandage and some "boo-boo" kisses will make it OK. If you are always there to step in and warn them to "be careful" each time they try to master a new skill, they will develop a fear that the world isn't safe or that they can't make a good decision without you.

It is so difficult to watch your child make a mistake or get hurt physically or emotionally, but instead of being reactive, be proactive and talk about things like responsibility and safety ahead of time. Then, when a situation arises, be supportive, empathetic, and validating. Be there as their guide or coach without impeding their confidence to handle the world they live in.

Playing Independently

There are a lot of benefits to letting children play without being watched every second. As a mom, it pains me to think about it sometimes because I love my children so much and want to be a part of their lives in every way, but I know that isn't in their best interests.

A recent article published in *The Journal of Pediatrics*, that stemmed from Peter Gray's earlier work, talked about how the decline in children's independent play has led to more mental health challenges, such as anxiety and depression. He reiterated that "play promotes mental health." And I couldn't agree more. As parents, if we are trying to set our children up for success in all areas of their life, primarily their mental well-being, then play should be at the forefront in everything we/they do. Gray states in an article he wrote in 2011, "Children are designed, by natural selection, to play. Wherever children are free to play, they do. Worldwide, and over the course of history, most such play has occurred outdoors with other children. The extraordinary human propensity to play in childhood, and the value of it, manifests itself most clearly in hunter-gatherer cultures."

The decline of independent play is a serious problem that needs to be addressed and changed. Unless safety is a concern, try not to persuade or control your child's play, especially when it's independent, imaginative play. Allow them the space to determine the play agenda, the plot for the story, what character they want to act out, and if they want a playground to act as a pirate ship or an airplane. They may want to make up their own reality and the details of it, so try not to correct them if they are pretending that a lion makes an "oink, oink" sound. And if your child's play is "to be continued," let them leave their mess for an additional day until their play scenario is completed.

In Jonathan Haidt's book *The Anxious Generation*, he clearly outlines that "free play" is chosen and directed by the child. When a parent becomes involved, the play becomes "less free, less playful, and less beneficial" (p. 53).

As a work-from-home parent, I often need to write reports, create curriculum, check emails, record podcasts, or make phone calls with my clients. There are various blocks of time throughout my day when I need the house to be quiet and my children to be occupied so I can get work done. Some of this "work" even includes cooking, doing dishes, or putting away laundry. Other times I just need a short break from work and parenting altogether, and I need some space and quiet to gather more energy to get through the day. The truth is that parents need breaks. And breaks are necessary and healthy.

So I want to start by giving you permission to take breaks and tell you it's OK to let your children play independently without you. It is not your job to entertain your children all the time. There is no need to feel guilty for not playing with them every second of the day. In fact, it is mentally and emotionally healthy for them to play without you.

I also want to remind you that it is OK if your child gets bored. If they do, let them figure it out independently. I find my children get the most imaginative and creative when they are bored. I give them agency to make their own play. Yes, it's true that if children get too bored, they can get into mischief and disruptive behaviors sometimes start to surface, but that usually means they need more intellectual stimulation, body movement, or connection. If those needs are met, make sure your children are set up for success to keep busy. This might mean planning some activities or gathering materials in advance. I would set out some books, craft and art supplies, and a few games to give your child options. Older children can be given a list of possible ideas and can go find most materials on their own.

Independent play can start as early as infancy during tummy time, when children can learn agency and autonomy. The more they learn it at an early age, the more they will successfully learn the life skill of being independent. The benefits of independent play include learning social, communication, critical-thinking, and problem-solving skills, and fostering creativity and imaginative play. Independent play is vital to a child's development.

Parenting Tip: Implement an independent daily quiet time in a dimly lit room and either read books, play, or nap!

As a professional therapist and mom of two, I have years of experience coming up with creative activities that keep children busy for blocks of time without my complete attention or help. Here are my top thirty:

1. Build a fort
2. Put stickers in a sticker book (try to get some scratch and sniff!)
3. Paint or color in a book, on paper, or on a box
4. Play with a sensory bin or in the sink with water and toys
5. Play with sensory dough or sand
6. Build with blocks
7. Get a stamp set (or use fruit!) and stamp on a piece of paper
8. Hang party streamers on a doorway to make a laser zone
9. Make an empty toilet paper or paper towel roll maze for pom-poms
10. Play outside in dirt or sand
11. Make a racetrack on the floor and drive small cars on it
12. Unravel a giant rubber band ball
13. Play with magnetic letters on the fridge or garage door
14. Play Skee-Ball or make a mini ball pit with baskets and small plastic balls
15. Create a fun obstacle course
16. Play hopscotch or Hula-Hoop
17. Read books independently or read to stuffed animals
18. Play mini bowling
19. Play doctor with a doctor kit and dolls or stuffed animals
20. Play restaurant with play food and dolls or stuffed animals
21. Have a tea party with dolls or stuffed animals
22. Do an easy craft
23. Play inside a play tunnel or tent
24. Draw with sidewalk chalk

25. Make hand puppets on the wall with flashlights or a projector
26. Paint rocks
27. Blow bubbles
28. Play dress-up
29. Play a board game or put a puzzle together
30. Play musical instruments or have a dance party

What else would you add to this list?

Chapter 9

Play for the Overtired, Overwhelmed, and Overworked Parent

> "Imaginative play can make for a happy childhood."
>
> —Jerome Singer

I OFTEN HEAR PARENTS SAY THEY HAVE A DESIRE TO PLAY with their children but don't know how. They also frequently tell me they are too tired or don't have time to play. We have all been there. Your child asks you to play with them after a long, busy day, and you just don't have the energy. The last thing you want to do is play. But you have muster up any energy you can because you know it makes a big difference in your child's behavior, your stress levels, and your relationship with each other.

This chapter will give practical ways parents can incorporate play into their daily routine without using a lot of time, energy, or effort. It may surprise parents to read this, but playing with your child doesn't necessarily mean you have to actively play *with* them on the floor or have active dialogue. Sometimes being playful or sitting alongside them while they play is all they need. Being in the same room and intentionally and actively watching them play is good enough on those long, exhausting days.

Years ago, after speaking at an event, I was inspired by a mom

I met who had just had her second child. Her older child, a toddler, was displaying signs of acting out, understandably so. She didn't know how to respond or adapt to such a big life change.

As a mom, I can picture this life stage well. I still remember sitting in a rocking chair in my newborn son's room a few days after his birth, filled with all sorts of postpartum emotions. I was grateful beyond words for my new son but simultaneously felt guilty about my firstborn daughter because I felt like she was being ignored and forgotten. For three years, I had poured all of my time and energy into her, and all of a sudden it was taken away. Not all of it, but my newborn's needs took precedence in those first couple weeks, and it was more than I could handle. My daughter would ask me to play with her, and I was either too busy or too tired. I said no a lot, and I hated myself for it. But what is a mom of more than one child supposed to do? No one prepared me for those moments as a mother, and nobody told me how hard it would be going from one child to two.

After this newly postpartum mom heard me speak, she went home that night and played. While she was holding her newborn child in a rocking chair, she played with her older daughter without having to move much or get off the chair. They were playing princesses, and she wore a crown on her head and waived a wand with her free hand while her daughter played next to her on the floor. She didn't have to stop holding the baby or even get up from the chair. She just had to put on a crown and play ever so slightly with the little energy she had.

I often compare play with going to the gym. I'll speak for myself here: Sometimes it takes all my willpower to go to the gym. I often feel like I don't have the energy or the time. But once I go to the gym, I feel so much better, have ample energy, and somehow still have time to complete most of my to-do list. Play has a similar effect.

Life is stressful and complicated, and there are a million things on our to-do lists that we consider more important than play. Our mental load alone inhibits play. And when you combine our mental load with physical exhaustion, play isn't even a remote priority. But I promise you, when you play, you will get energy. And you will find that you can make the time. You will feel more connected and attached to your child, and you'll start craving playtime more and more. Play is a bridge between you and your child, and researchers have found that playing helps stimulate all six feel-good hormones: endorphins, oxytocin, dopamine, norepinephrine, GABA, and serotonin. So prioritize play more often and glean all the benefits it offers.

How to Play when You're Exhausted

When you're feeling overtired, overwhelmed, and overworked, there are still many ways to play with your child. These are the times you need to think outside the box for ideas to connect and engage with your child in a playful way that doesn't require much energy. Here are a few ideas.

Spa

One of my favorite play-based ways to play when I'm exhausted is having my daughter play "spa" with me. I lie down on the couch with the lights dimmed, and she paints my nails, brushes my hair, reads me books, and puts cucumbers on my eyes. She will also play relaxing music for me from a media device. I am an active participant by playing with her, but I get to relax, close my eyes, and get pampered, which takes little to no energy. In fact, I sometimes get some energy back because I get a moment of rest, which comes in handy if she asks me to pamper her, too!

Doctor

Similar to the spa idea, lie down on the couch and be your child's patient. I suggest investing in a play medical kit. Not only can you use this kit for this activity, but it can be very useful for your children to understand medical checkups and play out their anxiety about going to the doctor. During this activity, your child can take your temperature, check your blood pressure, and listen to your heartbeat with the play stethoscope. Children love to play doctor, and you can rest as the sick "patient" they can help. This activity can also help children learn empathy.

Showtime

You can also ask your children to put on a show for you. Young children love to perform, sing, and dance. This way, you can sit down and be present enough to watch, but you don't have to actively play or participate with them.

Fashion Show

I give my son credit for this playful idea. When you are exhausted but want to play with your children, have them put on a fashion show for you. You can sit down on the couch or even on your bed and relax while they try on a variety of clothes from a dress-up box, their own room, or even your closet. Children love to play dress-up and especially love exploring your closet and pretending to be you, their hero and greatest role model! Sometimes, when my children play this game, they turn the overhead lights down and use a flashlight to make a spotlight for the sibling who's on the imaginary runway.

Story Time

Children love to get creative and use their imagination. Sit together on the couch and have your child tell you a story. When I have done this in the past, my children get so into it, they dress up like their character and also get props from around the house to use in their story. While you relax and sit back, they do all the work. All you have to do is make eye contact and listen so they know you are present. Children can come up with elaborate stories that can take a bit of time, so get comfy and let them take you on a journey into their creative mind. This activity can also work if your child can read. Have them sit alongside you and practice reading a book to you, or you can act it out while they are reading.

Indoor Scavenger Hunt

One of my favorite activities to do with my children on a busy and exhausting day is also intellectually stimulating and keeps their body moving: an indoor scavenger hunt. You can either make a list of things for them to find independently around the house (for example, a hairbrush, a spoon, a sock, a shoe, a book, a ball, and a stuffed animal), or create a list that helps them get out energy (for example, go into the backyard and do ten jumping jacks, go into the bedroom and spin five times, then use a stool to climb safely in the pantry and grab the peanut butter and cracker snack, which also helps motor skills). While they complete the list, I can rest on the couch.

Dance Party

I have talked about this before to break up a power struggle or a tantrum. But this also works when you are too tired to engage in play with your child on a busy or exhausting day. Just put on some music and invite your child to dance and show you their best moves while you watch.

Find a Way to Fit It in and Make It Work

Sometimes we have days where our only choice is to multitask. On these extra busy days, our only choice is to find a way to fit in play and make it work. So while you are making dinner, doing the dishes, or folding laundry, despite your physical and mental exhaustion, find a way to fit play in somehow. Remember, a little play goes a long way. Set your child up at a table near you with some modeling dough, toys, books, or crafts and let them play while you work. You can engage with them by asking them to make specific items out of the dough so you can actively play and participate together. This activity can also be done with drawing. Ask your child to draw a specific animal, food, toy, place, or person so you are actively engaged with them and their play while you work. They know you are present, which helps enhance your attachment and connection with them, even though you are working and not sitting next to them. In this scenario, you are consciously connecting through your presence.

Playing with your child is about intentionality. Whether you're listening to music together, having a dance party in the kitchen, or reveling in a game of Would You Rather, you are connecting and communicating. Though there are tasks you need to get done, these tasks don't usually need your full attention, so you can play at the same time!

PART III

Understanding and Conquering Common Childhood Behaviors

Chapter 10

Using Play to Help Your Child Self-Regulate

> "Play is often talked about as if it were a relief from serious learning. But for children play is serious learning. Play is really the work of childhood."
>
> —FRED ROGERS

CHILDREN BECOME DYSREGULATED FOR A VARIETY OF REASONS but, "In play, children learn to regulate their emotions" (Gray, 2011). This chapter will provide reasons why children dysregulate as well as quick, practical, and effective ways parents can help themselves and their children regulate by using play-based coping tools.

First and foremost, before you can effectively help your child self-regulate, you need to be regulated. Have you ever noticed that your child may be more dysregulated when you are dysregulated yourself? It's the chicken-and-egg scenario. It honestly doesn't matter which one came first in this case. Did you trigger your child or did your child trigger you? When either the parent or the child is activated and becomes dysregulated, the other one reacts and responds with the same energy. The cycle continues with escalation in both directions until, ultimately the parent starts yelling and the child starts crying, or vice versa. It's a difficult cycle to break when both the parent and the child are emotionally elevated. The goal for change is for both parent and child to effectively tolerate distress, form realistic expectations when a problem or disruption arises, and co-regulate.

Let's discuss for a moment what dysregulation is and what it looks like. Emotional dysregulation is when an individual's emotional state is disrupted by a major shift in mood and overwhelming and intense emotions that are difficult to control. Emotional dysregulation is characterized by the rigid inability to respond and manage your emotional state, which results in an intense and long-lasting emotional reaction that deviates from typically accepted social norms.

Dysregulation can look like numbness or inattentiveness; hyperfocus, hyperarousal, or hypersensitivity; elevated anxiety; or tantrums and meltdowns, evidenced by yelling, screaming, crying, stomping, or physical harm to self or others. It can also look like depression and self-isolation, loss of interest in usually pleasurable activities, emotional detachment, and disrupted sleeping or eating patterns. Physiological symptoms include an accelerated heart rate, headache, stomachache, or sweaty palms.

Before using the coping strategies in this book, make sure you, the parent, are in a calm and controlled state of mind. Maybe you're dysregulated because you have a lot on your plate, are sleep deprived, or just got into an argument with your spouse or your boss. Whatever the reason, justified or not, your child may not know or understand, so despite the challenges you are experiencing, give yourself permission to feel dysregulated for a few moments, then quickly and intentionally work toward emotional regulation. Remember that you are in control of your emotions, thoughts, and behaviors. Those three things are not in control of you.

The Dialectical Behavioral Therapy model uses a term called the wise mind. The wise mind sits nicely between the emotional mind and the rational or reasonable mind, overlapping slightly on both sides.

The emotional mind is the state of mind you are in when you act on your emotions in an impulsive and volatile way. You react on your urges quickly and without thinking about the outcome of your actions. The rational or reasonable mind uses facts, logic, and laser focus to solve a problem and respond slowly to a situation. When you respond, you may even feel emotionally numb, detached, and robotic. You may even minimize or avoid emotions completely, especially if you feel too vulnerable, and it's a way you try to protect yourself.

The wise mind takes both sides into account before responding. You acknowledge your emotional side as well as the facts about the situation before thoughtfully responding. Your response is balanced with clarity and mindfulness.

I am all about micro-mindfulness practices that I can easily sprinkle into my day. I have learned various ways over the years to take a moment here and there to rejuvenate and recharge rather than wait for a big chunk of time to relax.

How to Be Mindful to Help your Child

Now let's talk about how you can get into your wise mind before helping your child emotionally regulate. It's the same mentality of putting on your airplane oxygen mask before putting one on your child. Here are some quick and easy ways to help the regulation process.

Parent Time-Out

Give yourself grace and permission to take a break. Walk into another room or outside for a moment and take a few deep belly breaths while lifting your arms over your head and stretching. The fresh air, sunlight, and change of environment along with these body movements should help calm you down quickly.

Stimulate Your Sensory Receptors

Splash some cool water on your face, dab your face with a cold washcloth or wet wipe, or use a cool face roller. You can also rinse your hands under cold water. Other ways to stimulate your sensory receptors are brushing your hair; putting lotion on your hands; or giving yourself an arm, leg, or back scratch. You can also slowly drink some cold water or mindfully eat a small piece of chocolate. I keep a special sensory stash of chocolate just for myself in the pantry, out of reach from my children, for just these emergency occasions.

Deep Breathing

Deep breathing is the quickest and easiest calming method to use because you can do it anywhere at any time, and no one will know you are doing it except for you. Start by slowly breathing in through your nose, hold for five seconds, and then slowly breathe out through your mouth for five seconds. Repeat these steps until you feel calm and back to baseline. There are many different breathing techniques out there, so use the one that works best for you.

Mindfulness Body Scan

Put on some soft, calming music. Start at the top of your head and pause to mindfully notice each part of your body all the way down to your feet. Stay as present as you can without getting distracted.

Shoulder Tapping

This is one of my favorite somatic therapy calming exercises to regulate stress. Begin by placing your right hand on your left shoulder and your left hand on your right shoulder. Then gently tap one hand at a time on each shoulder in a consistent and rhythmic pattern. This bilateral stimulation exercise is very effective and has been practiced for a long time to help soothe the body.

Wellness Wink Breaks

How many times have you heard someone suggest you "pause and take a break"? Mental health professionals are constantly urging moms to check in with themselves, but how? How do we stop what we are doing to take a break? What does that even look like? My favorite way to pause in my own life is to set a timer on my phone that goes off periodically throughout the day. I have an alert midmorning and late afternoon (right before the witching hour and the final stretch of the evening hustle). I call these alert reminders wellness winks.

During these wellness winks, I ask myself a few questions like: When is the last time I ate food or drank water? When is the last time I went to the bathroom? Have I been outside yet today? Have I moved my body or exercised today? Do I need to ask for help or delegate a responsibility? Once I check in with myself and answer these quick questions, I can proactively meet my physical and mental needs. Sometimes we get so busy throughout the day, we forget to do simple things like go to the bathroom or drink liquids (other than coffee and energy drinks). And as the day goes on, our mental load gets louder and heavier, so try a wellness wink and see if it helps you regulate.

Journaling or Diary Dump

Journaling doesn't have to take a long time. Just write long enough to dump your stressors so they are moved from inside your mind to the paper. What you write doesn't even have to be in full sentences or spelled correctly. You can simply write bullet points of what is stressful. Or do the opposite and write out a few things you are grateful for in your life. The point is to externalize your emotions and thoughts.

Why Do Children Get Dysregulated?

The most common reasons children get dysregulated include:

- Environmental overstimulation
- Denial of access

- Environmental changes
- Sensory deprivation
- Emotional invalidation, abandonment, and rejection
- The Anxiety–Emotional Regulation Connection

Environmental Overstimulation

In my experience, the most common reason children get dysregulated is environmental overstimulation. The combination of lack of sleep and hunger with a busy schedule, too much time on the go, or extended time with others (we all need to recharge and rest even if we are extroverts who love to stay active) often results in emotional dysregulation. Sometimes school alone is an environmental trigger. The environment may be too loud, too bright, or too busy. Think of being at a theme park after multiple hours on a hot, busy day. The lines are long, and you haven't had anything to eat or drink in several hours. Your feet hurt and your head is starting to ache. Patience is running low, and your frustration tolerance is rapidly depleting. Picture what that looks and feels like for a moment. Can you feel your body tensing? What you are picturing in your mind, combined with what your body is feeling, is the overwhelming feeling children get when they are dysregulated. Can you blame them? And most times it doesn't take a long, busy day at a theme park.

Denial of Access

The second most common reason children get emotionally dysregulated is because they are denied access to something they want. In other words, they are told their favorite word, no (sarcasm intended). Whether it's because they want a cookie before dinner or they want five more minutes of screen time, they want their way and, in their mind, that is the only way. Some children, especially very young children, cannot cognitively comprehend why in the world you aren't saying yes to them. They are developmentally in a very ego-centric, self-absorbed developmental stage in their lives and honestly cannot wrap their brains around your rejection. In these moments, you may get an "I hate you" or "You are ruining my life" response, but at least they are using their words to try to express their big feelings in a way that makes sense to them. Deep down they don't mean it; they're just emotionally dysregulated.

Environmental Changes

Another common reason children become dysregulated is due to environmental changes. When a parent comes to me and says their child is acting up emotionally, one of the first questions I ask is whether anything changed in their environment recently. Did the family just welcome a new sibling? Did they move homes or change schools? Did the parents just separate or get divorced? Did a family pet or family member die recently? I'm sure the list could go on, but these are the main environmental changes that typically occur in a child's young life. And these environmental changes, although common and sometimes unavoidable, can cause major disruptions, affecting their emotionality and behavior.

Sensory Deprivation

Sensory deprivation is another reason children become dysregulated. So many of us regulate through our senses, and if we aren't able to activate our senses or cannot properly sensory seek to soothe, then we can emotionally dysregulate. Children, especially sensory seeking children, find this to be the biggest trigger of all.

Emotional Invalidation, Abandonment, and Rejection

Children get dysregulated because of emotional invalidation, abandonment, and rejection. If a child feels invalidated, rejected, or abandoned physically or emotionally by a parent or a peer, they can easily be triggered and become dysregulated. Being left alone on the playground or getting into an argument with a peer can trigger a young child significantly. On the same note, if they feel like they are unloved, even if it's just perceived, this may set off emotional dysregulation. This often happens when a parent is busy with daily tasks, such as paying bills, doing laundry, or making dinner, and the child believes they aren't getting enough attention. If a child asks a parent to play and the parent responds that they can't because they are busy, this could set off emotional dysregulation. If a parent is not connecting with their child in a mindful, present way, the child will feel they are being rejected. Perceived or temporary abandonment also comes into play when a parent has to go to work and the child is left with a babysitter or is dropped off at school, or when the parents go out of town. This could also be classified as separation anxiety, but either way, the child ends up emotionally dysregulated.

The lack of emotional validation can also dysregulate children when:

- They are taught that their emotions are wrong.
- They are shamed for their emotions.
- They feel they are unable to trust their emotions.
- They are unable to regulate their emotions.
- Their emotions are not validated.
- Their emotions are mocked.

Go on a Bear Hunt of Emotions

A child who has emotional sensitivity or is on sensory overload may be quick to have big feelings over little things, high stress levels, and a slow return to baseline. Some children are more prone to this than others, and it's something to be mindful of as a parent. When your child is having big feelings, it's important to let them experience those emotions and not avoid them. Try not to get impatient, frustrated, or mad at them when they are expressing emotionality, or they will learn that emotions aren't safe. If they feel forced to come back to baseline when they aren't ready, they will learn not to trust their bodies and will feel shame. Show them support, allow them the opportunity to feel their emotions, and give them space to regulate without you rushing, forcing, shaming, or punishing them.

The Anxiety–Emotional Regulation Connection

Anxiety plays a fundamental role in emotional dysregulation. Anxiety can single-handedly alter a child's mood, behavior, and functioning. Anxiety can include generalized anxiety, separation anxiety, or social anxiety.

One of the biggest reasons I have seen children emotionally dysregulate is because of separation anxiety. I previously had a client who had a tremendous amount of separation anxiety about going to school, which in turn caused a tremendous amount of emotional dysregulation. The typical behaviors you'd expect existed. The child would power-struggle and tantrum when getting dressed in the morning, cried each morning at drop off as well as sporadically throughout the day, and refused to participate in activities in the classroom or on the playground. The crying became so prominent, the school sent the child home early on multiple occasions. When it became almost unmanageable, I received a call. I was asked to intervene at the school as well as support the family at home.

I used play to work with the child on separation anxiety. I would take the child's stuffed animals and pretend they were classmates at school together. During our play, some of the animals would be shy and not very talkative. One of the animals would inevitably end up crying in the middle of our make-believe classroom, and another animal would come along and ask the crying child what was wrong. The tearful child would say something like, "I miss my mom and dad and just want to go home." Then another animal, acting as a heroic friend, would help the crying child. They would share various coping suggestions for the child to try—like slowly counting to ten or taking deep, cleansing breaths—and remind the child they would see their parents again soon. After role-modeling this a few times for my client, who was only four years old, they started repeating the same helpful tips to the stuffed animal through play. Shortly after this client learned how to control their emotions, build confidence, and learn various calming techniques, the separation anxiety stopped.

The Red/Green Card Game

If you are trying to teach your child to identify when they are dysregulated, try the red/green card game. It's fun and easy to play. Get two pieces of construction paper—one red and one green—or take two white pieces of paper and color them. Then front-load your child and teach them what each color means. Green means regulated and red means dysregulated. Thoroughly explain to them in age-appropriate terms what green means and what red means. You can give them a few examples of what being regulated and dysregulated looks and feels like.

If the child is emotionally regulated, you can sporadically hold up the green card so they know what regulated looks and feels like, in the hope that they can imitate that and repeat it in future circumstances. If the child is emotionally dysregulated, you can hold up a red card so they also know what emotional dysregulation looks and feels like. You don't have to stop what you are doing or say anything. Just hold up the card, and they will know how they are regulating based on the color of the paper. I love this exercise because it really helps a child become aware of their bodies, their emotional state, and how to be in control of themselves.

Sensory Avoiders or Sensory Introverts

One of the best ways you can help a child emotionally self-manage their behavior in a supportive, encouraging, and positive way is to stay calm and be prepared. This is when we want to co-regulate with them. This means we model regulation, coach through regulation, and even mirror regulation. The point being, you co-regulate with your child to strengthen your connection in a supportive and loving way. This is when you say "I'm here for you and I'm going to help you. We will do this together." When a child's behavior is escalated, it is often too late to wing it—you'll only do yourself and the child a disservice.

If your child is struggling with anxiety and it's affecting their emotional regulation, here are some general play-based solutions to help their symptoms. These strategies are more for sensory avoiders—or what I sometimes call sensory introverts—which are those children who are sensitive to loud noises and get dysregulated or overstimulated easily in busy environments. But they can be used for all children, depending on what will help calm their nervous system and return them to baseline or emotional balance. Finding the best regulation strategy for your child is a little like being Goldilocks, searching for the strategy that provides neither too much nor too little sensory stimulation, but just the right amount.

Play-Based Visual Imagery

This sensory experience only takes a few moments, and it's very powerful. First have the child think of their happy place or a happy memory. You can have them imagine their favorite activity—like playing on the swings, swimming in the pool, or visiting the zoo. In a soft, slow, calm voice, describe the activity in detail, and have your child imagine the smell, sounds, and other senses while you are talking. I often use the beach for this intervention. Have the child explore their five senses to think of everything they see, hear, smell, taste, and touch. Have them imagine how the sand feels between their toes. Is it warm or cool on their feet? What do the ocean waves sound like? Do they hear laughter? Seagulls? Do they smell someone having a barbeque? Do they see children playing Frisbee or beach volleyball? Is it busy or quiet? Is it hot or breezy? Are there a lot of clouds or is it almost sunset? You can also have your child imagine their favorite stuffed animal or toy that they love to play with and go through the same sensory exercise.

Grounding Exercises

Have your child sit or lie down comfortably with their eyes closed. Ask them to take two or three deep breaths—in through the nose, out through the mouth. Then ask your child to slowly open their eyes and tell you two things they see, two things they smell, two things they hear, two things they can touch, and two things they taste (this can be imaginary). Then end this exercise by taking another two or three deep breaths.

Or have your child go outside with no shoes on. Ask your child to walk around the grass or concrete and feel the sensory effects of their experience. What do they see? What do they smell? What do they feel?

Tangible Toys

Find sensory-friendly toys that provide an emotional, physical, and mental release that your child can see, touch, or smell. Do they have a favorite blanket, pillow, or stuffed animal? Maybe they like Play-Doh or Silly Putty or a punching bag or ball. Have the child intentionally play with this toy-based item and describe how it feels when they touch it, how it smells, and what it looks like by using as many descriptive words as possible.

Affirmations

Here are some affirmations you can try to help empower your child when they are feeling emotionally dysregulated:

> I am going to try my best today.
> If I need a break, I will ask for one.
> If something is difficult, I won't quit.
> I will have a positive attitude.
> All I need to do is try.
> I haven't done it yet, but I will.
> I am proud of myself for giving it my all.
> I will be the best I can be today.
> I will get through difficult moments.
> I am capable.
> I believe in myself.
> I have the strength to overcome any challenge.

Chase the Blues and Greens . . . Outside

Nature therapy, or ecotherapy, has a positive impact on a child's mental health because fresh air and spending time outdoors are known to improve the immune system, relieve stress, and release mood-boosting hormones like serotonin and dopamine. In color therapy, also known as chromotherapy, looking at shades of blue and green can help reduce stress and anxiety. The calming effects of certain colors are a cornerstone of color therapy. So go outside and "chase the blues and greens" with your child!

Playing in nature also helps children develop better posture, balance, coordination, and body awareness. And playing in dirt has emotional and physical benefits, too. Soil has healthy bacteria that can build the immune system, and some plants, such as sage, lavender, pine, and citrus, also produce natural stress relief chemicals called terpenes. And don't forget all the physical and mental health benefits of vitamin D.

Studies have shown that if you go outside for at least three minutes early in the day and look in the direction of the rising sun, you will gain exposure to solar blue light. This can help maintain the body's circadian rhythm, which regulates a body's natural wake and sleep cycles and keeps us alert during the day. It also signals the body to release serotonin, a hormone that contributes to our sense of well-being, helps memory and brain function, and elevates mood. Solar blue light is also important for the growth and development of eyes and vision in children.

Need a nature walk in the evening? I suggest going on a witching hour walk, which typically happens in the second half of the day, when you notice tension in your home rising. Take this time to go on a walk in the neighborhood. The change in temperature and environment, mixed with movement and fresh air, should start to regulate everybody's system quickly.

Nature Scavenger Hunt

Take a nature walk a step further and make it into a nature scavenger hunt, one of my favorite play-based activities to help a child have fun and simultaneously self-regulate. This activity combines play, movement, fresh air, nature, art, and teamwork, all while connecting with your child. When emotions are high, take your child outside on a nature scavenger hunt and have them collect various items like leaves, branches, rocks, and flowers. When you get home, they can play with or paint their treasures. If they collect flowers, they can create a beautiful bouquet, or they can glue their treasures together to make a collage. They can even play with their treasures at the table or in the backyard and make a pizza out of what they found, including dirt for the sauce, rocks for the pepperoni, and sticks for the peppers.

Send It Down the River

I need to give my husband credit for this intervention. It's such a beautiful way to visualize releasing toxic emotions that are inhibiting a child from being regulated. First, it is important that a child acknowledges the negative emotion or thought they are experiencing. A child should name the emotion and sit in the emotion for a few moments. During this time, you can physically console your child and validate their emotions. You can let them know it is common to feel this emotion and it's OK to express it. Then teach them to let it go. A child can picture a river in their mind, and when a debilitating thought or emotion invades their mind or body's space, they can pretend to take that emotion or thought off their body and place it in the river. Once it starts drifting down the river, they watch that thought or emotion float away, which figuratively releases toxic tensions from their body. This is a great way to externalize emotions and thoughts, using visual imagery to release and let go of them in order to regulate.

Let the Lanterns Go

My daughter came up with this intervention. It's similar to the river intervention, but she put her own spin on it. We were talking about being in control of our emotions, thoughts, and behaviors, and how we can use thought stopping, a cognitive behavioral therapy intervention, to stop negative thoughts and replace them with more positive ones. She took it to the next level and said that when she has a negative thought, she puts it on a Chinese lantern and sends it away in the air, where it has the potential to float far away. Genius, right? A child can visually picture themselves putting a negative thought onto a lantern and having it float away (you can use a balloon as a replacement for the lantern). They can easily imagine what the lantern or balloon looks like as it drifts away until it is finally gone. Once the lantern or balloon is out of their imaginary sight, the negative thought or feeling should be, too.

The Washing Machine

Out of all the interventions I have done with children, this has to be the winner. And it's a sensory hack many parents don't even know exists. If your child is struggling with emotional dysregulation, overstimulation, sensory seeking, or other physical behaviors and needs a calming mechanism, try "the washing machine." Get a bed sheet and have your child climb inside (make sure their head shows so they can breathe well). For younger children, you can "wash" them by rolling them around on the ground and pushing on pressure points so their sensory receptors are activated. Older children can roll around on their own. And don't forget the spin cycle, when you pick them up and spin them around in a few circles while they're inside the sheet. Even if your child isn't struggling with sensory seeking or emotional regulation, children will love the washing machine. It's a playful activity for parents to do with their children and a fun way to get the wiggles out before bed.

Expandable Sphere

A colorful toy expandable sphere is one of my favorite tools to teach children regulation. It's an effective way to teach children deep breathing techniques to control their body. A child can use this sphere to practice deep breathing. The sphere matches their breath and is a physical manifestation of how to control their breath. When the sphere expands, they inhale slowly through their nose, and when it closes, they exhale slowly out of their mouth.

Bubbles and Feathers

Another way to teach children playful deep breathing is by using a feather or bubbles. Have the child inhale and exhale the feather up and down, or blow the bubbles in and out. This exercise is a tangible, visual, and physical manifestation of the breath.

Stress Squeezes

A child can playfully regulate by squeezing a stuffed animal or a stress ball. Children should squeeze in slow, rhythmic motions until they are calm.

Weighted Blanket or Stuffed Animal

A great way to help regulate a child is by using a weighted blanket or weighted stuffed animal. The heaviness of the blanket or stuffed animal helps a child feel safe and secure. For safety purposes, supervise your child with a weighted blanket and make sure they have a weighted blanket specifically for children so it's not too heavy and they can't get trapped underneath and suffocate. Weighted stuffed animals are typically two to five pounds but your child should still be monitored if they are young.

Self-Regulation Station

This is the most popular intervention I use with my clients. This exercise helps a child recognize their emotions and self-regulate their behaviors. When choosing a self-regulation station area in your home, let the child have a say in where it will be located, and have them help you decorate it. Also, since it isn't used punitively, when you suggest your child go to the self-regulation station to calm their body, offer to go there with them rather than just sending them away to be alone. You can either sit near them for support or actively help them regulate with the items in the station.

So how does the self-regulation station work? First, decide how many cool-down periods you want the child to have each day and create break cards for them. A break card is a card you can create for your child that they can use as a ticket to pause what they are doing or to take a break. You can just write the words "Take a break" on a piece of paper, or get more elaborate and add clip art of a child holding their hand up or a stop sign and laminate them for multiple uses. When your child feels their emotions starting to escalate (or you observe this), teach them to take a break card and give it to you or place it in a designated spot. When they give you a card, praise them for identifying and taking control of their emotions. Try to limit their time in the self-regulation station with a sand timer so they only stay there for five to ten minutes. Once they use their designated number of cards each day or their time is up inside, encourage them to use other coping skills in their toolbox for the remainder of the day. Use the cards and area as long as you find necessary. Experiment with how many cards to use per day and how long the child needs in the self-regulation station. This exercise is neither a punishment nor a reward but a time to calm themselves in their safe haven.

How to Build a Self-Regulation Station

Here are some items you can have in the self-regulation station:

- Sensory bottles
- Crayons and paper
- Pillow and blanket (blue/green calming colors)

- Play-Doh
- Five- to 10-minute sand timer
- How to Be A Superhero Called Self-Control book
- Soft classical music
- Soothing scents (lavender, for example) from rice bags or essential oils
- Scratch-and-sniff stickers
- Lotion or a brush
- Back scratcher
- Play tunnel or sensory sack
- Punching bag
- Fidgets

Sensory Seeking Regulation for Sensory Extroverts

Do you have a sensory seeking child—or what I like to sometimes call a sensory extrovert—at home? How do you know if you do? If your child is constantly moving and always seems to have a ton of energy at all hours of the day, can't seem to slow their brain or body down, yells often, or loves loud sounds and vibration, you may have a sensory seeking child. Do you have a child who seems to be dysregulated or overstimulated a lot? Do they rarely appear calm? Do they constantly crave sensory input? Do they repeatedly want to touch you or other people? These also may be signs of a sensory seeking child. Typically, sensory seeking children love to be touched and even have the need to be compressed. Tactile touch is their love language. Sensory seeking children also may have trouble focusing, appear hyperactive, express impulsivity, and prefer adrenaline-related activities.

You may ask why your child is sensory seeking. And the answer is mostly due to the way their brain processes their senses and the sensations their body receives. Basically, your child is sensory seeking to regulate. If a child cannot mentally and physically process the sensory input their body is receiving, they seek it more until their body is satisfied. This is primarily due to vestibular sensory processing. This is why you will often see sensory seekers doing a significant amount of extreme physical activity, such as jumping, running, climbing, and even squeezing everyone and everything in sight or crashing into objects and people. The more extreme the activity and energy it takes to do the activity, the better. It seems counterintuitive, but to calm a sensory seeking child, it will take higher energy than their norm. Deep breathing, meditation, and other calming activities usually don't work. Some sensory seekers can control their need for stimulation and movement in various environments. Others cannot.

Here are some ways to help a sensory seeking child regulate.

Obstacle Course

My favorite play-based way to fulfill a child's sensory needs and regulate them is an obstacle course. The movement, the fulfillment of tactile stimulation, the successful ways the body and brain are receiving sensory input, and the satisfaction of happy sensory receptors all over their body makes this activity ideal. Sensory seeking children desire an abundant amount of adrenaline-related actions and crave a significant amount of sensory input (like loud music, vibration, climbing, jumping, or squeezing). If a child cannot mentally and physically process the sensory input their body is receiving, they seek it more until their body is satisfied. Your obstacle course can be small and mighty or elaborate and challenging. Combine things like hopscotch, Hula-Hoops, sensory stones, play tunnels, and other textured objects for your child to experience and master as they travel through the obstacle course.

Jumping Jacks

Who remembers having to do jumping jacks during P.E. in middle school? I hope I am not alone, but it was never a favorite activity of mine. But sensory seeking children love the movement and the pressure of jumping. They also benefit from the sensory receptors in their hands and feet being stimulated. Plus, jumping jacks take energy, so children tire out their bodies while calming their minds. It seems counterintuitive to do more physical activity to calm down, but even if this is done before bedtime, your child is more likely to sleep better!

Pro Tip: *If your child doesn't respond well to jumping jacks, try a small indoor trampoline or moving up and down on an exercise ball! If you don't want to go that route, your child can get a similar sensation by jumping off the bed or couch.*

Joint Compression

This is one of my favorite ways for children to get their sensory seeking behaviors met. A few ways you can meet this need through joint compression are via a sensory sock, a pressure massage, tight bear hugs, a calming tunnel, or a weighted blanket. All of these work really well for children who want to feel pressure or release pressure. Try giving your child a deep pressure massage on their arms and legs, then see if they can return the favor—it's a parenting win!

Pro Tip: *Don't have these play tools at home? You can also use a pillow or stuffed animal to squeeze.*

Sensory Bins

Sensory bins are one of my favorite ways for children to use their senses and soothe. There are endless ways to play with a sensory bin. The more varying textures you have in your bin, the better. You can even make them themed based on your child's interests, such as animals, insects, or dinosaurs. Fill the bin with dried rice, dried beans, dried pasta, dried oats, unpopped popcorn, or water beads, then add in items like cotton balls, pom-pom balls, glitter, buttons, feathers, magnetic letters, puzzle pieces, action figures, foam blocks, clothespins, shells, and other small toys. Then add small cups, funnels, tongs, spoons, empty toilet paper rolls, empty paper towel rolls, or even an ice cube tray. Allow the space to get messy. Everything, including your child, can get cleaned up. The messier, the better sensory experience for them, which is the point.

You can take a sensory bin to the next level by making it water- or sand-based. Playing with water and sand is soothing to the touch and activates the sensory system on multiple levels. I suggest getting a mini pool and filling it with a small amount of water and some toys of various textures. Have your child play in it while touching and exploring all the toys. Don't forget items like a funnel or a cup so they can watch the water go in and out like a waterfall. Need something on a smaller scale? Try putting water and some toys in a sink or bathtub for a water play sensory experience.

Pro Tip: *For sand play, have your child play in the sandbox in the backyard. You can also head to the beach or to a local park that has a sandy area. Just don't forget to bring shovels, sifters, and scoops!*

Scooter Board

Scooter boards are great for children seeking sensory stimulation. They can lie on their belly and scoot around the house, backyard, or driveway (with supervision of course). Not only will it tire them from the movement, but it also will meet their sensory needs. Scooter boards offer an entire body experience. Don't forget a helmet for safety!

Pro Tip: *Don't have a scooter board handy? Let your child roll around on a skateboard or rolling cart for a similar effect. You can also have them ride in a wagon or stroller.*

Musical Instruments

Music can be very soothing for children because they love exploring various sounds and vibrations that the instruments make. Children can play music with a mini piano, maracas, drums, tambourines, harmonica, triangle, cymbals, or even a ukulele! If you don't own any of these, grab some items around your home to make your own instruments, like using a spatula and a plastic bowl for drums. Although some sensory seeking children crave loud noise, others may be sensitive to noise, which can be over-stimulating and dysregulating, so stay in tune to your child's behavior while they play.

Slime and Sensory Dough

Playing, kneading, pulling, and poking slime or dough is an engaging activity for sensory seeking children. You can buy slime or dough premade, but making them at home is quick, easy, and simple. Make it extra fun by making slime with color-changing glue or glue with glitter. And sensory objects like pom-poms, beads, buttons, or dried macaroni to make it extra sensory activating!

Stuffed Animal Play

There are two fun ways to play with stuffed animals that will help activate the senses and regulate your child. First, have your child pick out a few preferred stuffed animals, and lie down in a safe, comfortable spot. Once they are still, take one stuffed animal and gently push it down to apply light pressure on different parts of their body—primarily their arms, legs, tummy, or the side of their face. This will help calm your child and provide sensory input in a fun, playful way through touch and tactile stimulation. If your child is in more of an active phase, put a group of stuffed animals on the floor and have your child jump off the couch into the pile. This will also help them feel grounded and regulated.

Chapter 11

Taming Tantrums and Managing Meltdowns

"Enter into children's play, and you will find the place where their minds, hearts, and souls meet."

—Virginia Axline

THIS CHAPTER WILL DISCUSS PREVENTIVE, PLAY-BASED STRATEGIES for how to manage and help lessen the duration and severity of tantrums and meltdowns. Although some tantrum behavior is developmentally expected at a young age and is typical for most children, there are still ways parents and caregivers can help manage them. Meltdowns can be a little more challenging but can also be controlled more effectively with the right coping tools.

The difference between tantrums and meltdowns is subtle, and the terms are often used interchangeably. A tantrum is typically less severe and more controlled in response to a minor and specific frustration, while a meltdown is often more severe and uncontrolled in response to extreme dysregulation. A tantrum is often shorter in duration and can be more easily stopped, while a meltdown lasts longer and is harder for a child to control.

When it comes to tantrums and meltdowns, being proactive and preventive is key. When a parent learns what sets off their child's behavior (typically denial of access to something, abrupt changes to the schedule, or transitions) they can be prepared and thoughtful about how they handle them in the future. And keep in mind, these big-feeling moments are often messy.

One of the best ways to be proactive about minimizing childhood tantrums is for parents to modify the language they use with their children. When parents avoid using words like no, don't, and stop, it alleviates some of the defensiveness and power struggles in children since these are trigger words. Parents can reframe how they say no to a child so it isn't taken defensively.

Here are some examples from negative language to positive language:

No yelling	"Use an indoor voice."	"Use your quiet voice."
Don't ignore me	"Put your listening ears on."	"Listen and look at me."
Stop running	"Please walk."	"Use walking feet."

Teach and show your child what *walking feet* looks like. Teach and show your child what *a quiet voice* sounds like. When you take the time to teach and show your child the *correct* way you want them to behave, they will be more likely to comply. This is the time to emphasize what you want your child to do (e.g., walk) instead of emphasizing what you don't want them to do (e.g., run). And make it playful. First yell a phrase and ask your child if that is using your indoor voice. Then try a different volume like whispering. Then use the correct tone. You can make this teaching moment fun. Let them tell you the difference between the volume of the voices—that is how they will remember it best—and you'll use play to strengthen your communication and connection along the way!

If your child is having a tantrum or meltdown, the key is not to overreact in the moment. Stay calm and know it will pass. The more you try to stop it, the worse it will get. When your child is already escalated, it is often too late to intervene. Their levels of cortisol, the stress hormone, are so high that their brains are foggy and they are unable to process logic or rationalize.

They are watching you for a reaction, so show them how to be calm and controlled. Role-model the behavior you want them to have. As difficult as it can be, especially in public, it is important to remain calm. Avoid giving in, shaming them, or punishing them for the emotions they are experiencing. Instead, acknowledge and validate the emotion while holding them accountable for their behavior. You also need to hold your ground and set a limit or boundary—for example, "You can be angry we aren't getting a toy today at the store, but it's not OK to scream and kick me, so to be safe, we are going to go to the car and leave." Then follow through and leave. Consistency is key so your intelligent children do not take advantage of any newly discovered loopholes.

I recommend that parents don't spend a lot of time directly paying attention to the behavior or actively trying to get their children to "stop." Instead, I suggest parents keep doing the activity they were doing. In this case, parents aren't actively ignoring; they are present and engaged but emotionally removed.

Managing Meltdowns Through Play

Try these play-based solutions to help prevent tantrums and meltdowns.

Quick Tips for Taming Tantrums and Managing Meltdowns

1. Know your child's triggers and plan for them. Maybe it's sharing, eating vegetables, or transitions. Make sure to let your child know in advance what to expect before a trigger is going to occur and make sure to give them the plan for how to handle their triggers. For example, let them know ahead of time what food to expect at mealtime, or teach and remind them what sharing is before they have a playdate.

2. Give children a means to express themselves without injuring themselves or you. Whether you use a self-regulation station, a punching bag, or a pillow, have a safe plan for when your child gets escalated.

3. Support them and let them know emotions are healthy to express in a safe, respectful, and responsible way. Teach them what different emotions are and how to use words or hand signals to share how they feel.

4. Try not to focus on the tantrum and negative behaviors as much as the positive behaviors and when your child is not having a tantrum. Notice and praise your child when they behave appropriately. You will feel more empowered when you focus on the solution, not the problem.

5. Try to figure out the motivation of your child's behavior before the tantrum begins. Are they tired or hungry? Are they having a tantrum because they want power or connection, or are they trying to avoid a task of some kind? Use a behavior chart to document patterns, triggers, timing, and the severity of their behavior.

6. Distract or redirect your child when a tantrum is starting to erupt. Give them space or fresh air. Put on some music and start dancing to deflect their attention. Start playing a game and see how quickly your child joins in.

Build Your Child's Frustration Tolerance

A low frustration tolerance will trigger emotional dysregulation. How well does your child handle frustrating situations? When they get offended or embarrassed, do they have a tantrum or a meltdown? When an upsetting situation comes up, is your child able to shake it off and move on fairly quickly, or do they ruminate and obsess over every little detail? Is your child easily triggered, or do they get irritable quickly? If so, they may have a low frustration tolerance and need extra support. To build their frustration tolerance, they need to experience situations that make them a tad uncomfortable—slowly, a little at a time. The best way to start this exposure and experience training is by role-modeling. Create a scenario that makes your child uncomfortable and have your child act out different roles and outcomes to experience the situation in different ways—one way with a low frustration tolerance and one way with a high frustration tolerance. Knowing what to expect and practicing their reaction in advance can help them experience it the same way when it really happens.

Schedule Tantrum Time

When your child is actively having a tantrum or meltdown, grab a sand timer and encourage them to express all their feelings for five to ten minutes, depending on their need. During this time, they can stomp, yell, whine, pace, roll around on the floor, or cry. Tell them you will be in the same room, doing something else while they engage in their behaviors. Continue to do what you need to do, then check in when time is up. Ask, "Would you like a hug, or do you need three to five more minutes on the timer?" Depending on your child's response, honor what they need. After the second check-in, say, "Are you ready to join me in the other room now? I was hoping we could play a board game." If your child refuses to join you right away, tell them you are going to start and they can join you when they are ready, which typically only takes a few minutes. Then play together and make it a positive, connected experience. Later, when your child is regulated and calm, you can reflect with them and ask them what they can do differently the next time they have big feelings, or ask if they need to make a repair with anyone and apologize for hitting, yelling, or biting. You shouldn't force your child to apologize but help increase their empathy and awareness of how their behaviors affected themselves and others. This awareness will help them take ownership and responsibility for their actions in future scenarios. You can also do this activity before an upcoming tantrum trigger in a controlled space to get the emotions out proactively and preventively before your child becomes dysregulated in an uncontrolled place.

Glitter Bottles

Imagine for a moment that a glitter bottle represents your child's dysregulation. The more overwhelmed and overstimulated your child becomes, the more the glitter swirls and twirls in every direction and your child starts behaving in maladaptive ways. The spinning glitter looks a lot like how your child's body and brain look like from the inside when they are having a tantrum or meltdown. On the other hand, when your child is calm, their brain and body are like the glitter that settles to the bottom of the bottle in a still state. This bottle is a great visual representation your child can comprehend, helping them become aware of their body when it is dysregulated. It can also be used as a calming mechanism when they are dysregulated. It only takes a few minutes and three ingredients to make: water, glitter, and bit of glue to keep the top closed.

Transitions

Many tantrums are caused because a child lacks the ability to handle a transition or a parent lacks the ability to offer transitions. Transitions can be challenging, especially when a child is actively participating in a preferred activity and they are asked to switch to a less-preferred activity. But don't worry, I have some play-based parenting hacks, tips, and tricks for you to try with your children in the hope they make transitions a little bit easier and smoother for you.

Set a Timer

Set a timer on your phone or microwave, or use a colorful sand timer. You can purchase an inexpensive set of timers with six different colors of sand representing time increments from thirty seconds to ten minutes. When you need your child to transition, tell them you are setting a timer for five minutes. Then let them know what to expect when the timer goes off, and tell them what they can look forward to when they transition. For example, if you are leaving the park to go home, tell them they can have a special snack in the car on the way or they can pick the songs to listen to during the ride home. Then place the timer near them so they can easily see or hear it. Once it goes off, be standing and ready to go. Remind them that the timer went off and it's time to leave. Then remind them of their special perk during the transition, ask them what they are going to choose, get excited about it, and leave.

Verbal Countdown

Many parents, including myself, use this common and effective approach for transitions. Basically, you tell your child they have ten minutes to complete their activity before they need to transition to the next activity. Let them know what is next so they can have ample processing time. Then every two minutes after that first warning, start counting down to eight minutes, six minutes, four minutes, two minutes, and then let them know time is up. Some children need proof, so the auditory or visual timers tend to work better here, but this tactic works well with most children.

Play It Out

For this tactic, make transitioning fun. For example, make leaving the park into a game. Ask your child to race you to the car, and whoever wins gets a special treat at home, extra time on the iPad, or additional time to stay up past their bedtime. If you or your child aren't into running races, hop to the car on one foot or move slowly like a sloth if you have time to spare. But make heading to the car fun regardless. You can also play freeze dance to the car. Put on their favorite song and tell them to dance to the car when they hear the song playing but freeze when the song stops. Do this until you reach the car. If you are transitioning at home from playtime to mealtime, just modify these games. For example, do freeze dance from the playroom to the kitchen or bathroom to wash their hands before mealtime.

Switch-a-Roo

If you want your child to transition smoothly, play a little switch-a-roo with them. Shift their attention from one activity to another activity they can look forward to. Then switch the power dynamic and ask them how much more time they need or want to play before transitioning as if they were the parent. They might say something outrageous like "a year" or "twenty hours," but remember that most children under ten don't know how to tell time very well and don't grasp the concept of time, so negotiate with them. If they say twenty minutes, respond, "How about ten minutes?" Maybe you'll settle at fifteen minutes. When they feel like they are part of the decision-making process, they are more apt to comply. Once time is up, shift their mindset from one activity to the next, then switch activities.

Ask "What Is Your Last Choice?"

When your child is about to transition, ask them the last thing they want to do before you leave or clean up. This question will empower your child and help them believe they are in charge of what they do before transitioning. When children feel like they have some sort of control over the situation they are less likely to protest. They might choose going down the slide one more time before you leave the park, or they might choose to draw one more picture before putting the paper and crayons away. If they can't think of something that won't take a long time, offer them options. Then let them choose one "last thing" to keep the empowerment moving in their favor.

Offer an Incentive

Incentives are so effective, especially when you need your child to comply and transition. First, set up a token system like pretend money, a sticker chart, points, or raffle tickets. Then set up the behavior expectation. Tell them if they listen and follow directions when you ask them to transition, they will earn a sticker for their chart, a raffle ticket, etc., which will ultimately earn them a bigger reward.

With these coping tools, tantrums and meltdowns are more easily managed and minimized.

Chapter 12

Helping Your Child Control Anger and Aggression

"Play is the highest form of research."

—ALBERT EINSTEIN

IN THIS CHAPTER, PARENTS WILL LEARN PLAY-BASED STRATEGIES to help manage their child's anger and aggression. I share simple ways parents can help their child identify, express, and process their big feelings in more positive ways. Children have strong emotions and often don't know what to do with them, so this will be a guide to help parents support their child through play.

All children are capable of anger and aggression outbursts. Are you even a child if you don't get angry or aggressive sometimes? Expressing anger is a way children learn about their bodies and how to control them, as well as how to effectively express and communicate their emotions, so some level of dysregulation is expected. Some children tend to be more aggressive than others due to their personality and temperament, and even if they have been exposed to this type of behavior at home or have a trauma history, but all children will have trouble controlling their anger from time to time. I find that many parents are scared of their child's anger and will bend over backward for their child just so they don't get angry, but that isn't healthy, either. Children need to express anger; they just have to learn how to express it in a healthy, positive, and effective way.

To understand anger and aggression, first a parent needs to know that anger is a secondary emotion. Primary emotions include feelings like sadness, fear, hurt, embarrassment, and worry. If a child is feeling one of these primary emotions, they may express it as anger.

It's like an onion peel that needs to be unraveled to get to the core. A child may be presenting with angry behavior, but in reality, underneath the anger, they are sad about something that happened at school that day or they are worried about something. Part of our job as parents is to be detectives and find out what underlying emotion caused the anger outburst. Sometimes, a child is simply angry because they're angry. They are denied access to something they want, which can trigger them emotionally with rage. This usually happens immediately after they are told no. But if your child has a prolonged mood swing or underlying irritability, that's when you might find out there is more to the behavior than meets the eye.

Let's start with emotional intelligence and how children identify their emotions. This is a very important step in how a child comprehends and expresses their emotions and behaves when a big feeling arises. If they can't identify what they are feeling, they will just express it impulsively in any form, not even knowing there may be other ways to control it. First, a parent needs to label emotions when they or their child are feeling them. Expand a child's vocabulary and understanding of each emotion as it's experienced. You can start with the most common basic emotions like happy, sad, scared, worried, and angry. I recommend labeling higher-level emotions as soon as your child conceptualizes them. If you are feeling frustrated, overwhelmed, embarrassed, or irritated, tell your child. Label it and define it. Explain how these emotions feel in age-appropriate terms. For example, "Mommy is embarrassed right now. Embarrassed feels a lot like when I do something that makes me feel like others will laugh at me or judge me for doing something silly." You can change the wording based on your child's age and developmental level.

Show your child what each emotion looks like and feels like. Many young children can't communicate what they are feeling and experiencing, which makes them even more frustrated because they perceive the adult as not understanding, validating, or empathetic. An adult may get frustrated because they don't understand, so they tell the child to stop and calm down, which only intensifies the cycle of miscommunication and behavior. This will lead to a child shutting down or engaging in a maladaptive behavior. When a child gets louder and angrier, it's typically because they aren't feeling heard. They aren't trying to make things worse, they just don't know how to say, "I'm hurt, and I just need you to listen and understand. I need your help." But in these cases, the intensified meltdown frustrates the parent, and the situation amplifies instead of calming down. So how do you stop the cycle?

Once you are able to label, define, and explain emotions, show your child how to handle the emotion in an effective and positive way. Role-modeling the behavior you want your child to have is key to how your child will actually behave. If you get angry and yell, that is what your child will learn and do when they are angry. A good scream is cathartic, but it needs to be controlled. If you want to let out a good scream, by all means do so, but prepare your child for it and do it in an appropriate place and time. Sometimes if I am angry, I tell my children I am angry and say, "You know what will make me feel better? A good yell. Let's go into the backyard and both scream at the top of our lungs and see how we feel afterward." Or I might say, "Let's get a pillow and hit it over and over as hard as we can and see if that helps us feel better." That way, it is premeditated and they know it's OK to be angry, but it's not uncontrollable because they can't regulate their body.

A mom friend recently told me that her elementary-aged daughter came home from school irritable, snapping back and displaying a negative and angry attitude. She said she normally would have just sent her to her room to cool down or taken away video games she covets as a punishment. But she had me in her ear and said she spent a few minutes playing a high five game with her instead. Out of the blue, she put her hand up for a high five but kept pulling her hand away when her daughter's hand would get close. She said she quickly started giggling, and it broke the angry mood she was in. Once she was calm, my friend asked her what was going on and she told her that she was hungry. Once she ate a snack, she was in a good mood for the rest of the day. Sometimes it just takes a small and simple shift in how we react to our children to replace an impulsive consequence because we've been ignited by their fire.

Processing Anger Through Play

Here are some other quick, play-based ways to express and process anger in a controlled, effective, and positive way to inspire behavior modification.

Bop Bag

One of my favorite ways to help children express and process their anger and aggression is through a bop bag or punching bag. Parents can teach their child to use a bop bag or a punching bag to hit or kick to let aggression out. Hitting and kicking something soft over and over again is very cathartic and will help your child regulate when they are having big emotions. It has so many therapeutic benefits as a way to release extra energy and is used as a replacement strategy for children who are hitting other family members and for those with sensory seeking behaviors.

Pillow

Similar to the bop bag, you can simply use a pillow to scream into, hit, stomp or jump on, or even throw it against the couch or wall. A pillow has so many functional uses for anger and aggression. Please supervise your children when they are using a pillow, especially when they are screaming into it, to prevent suffocation or hyperventilation. They should also be supervised if they are throwing it inside the house. I recommend having your child go to the store to pick out a special throw pillow of choice to use for just these occasions. They can pick the texture, color, and shape, and even write their name on it or color it.

Giant Sponge

Get a giant sponge, drench it, and allow your child to throw it on the ground as hard as they can in the backyard or driveway. Have your child do this exercise over and over as many times as they need to regulate. It incorporates water play while letting out anger and aggression, so the sensory boost is a bonus.

Dragon's Breath Game

Sometimes it is helpful for a child to play a game when they are upset. Have your child pretend they are a dragon by breathing in as big as they can, then letting out a loud breath that sounds and feels like dragon's fire. The child can even take it a step further and pretend they are breathing fire on various items around the house (not people or pets). They can be as loud as they want and will benefit from the vibrating sensation in their neck, which will help them feel strong and empowered. They will also learn how to release, control, and express their anger in an appropriate and fun way.

Scribble It Out

Let your child scribble their anger out. This type of exercise helps a child externalize anger on paper instead of having it swirling around inside of them. First, have them name the anger. Many of my clients will give it an actual name like Mark or Joe, or make up a code word for it like "bubbles" or "black cloud" or "lightning bolt" or "an ocean storm." Next have them draw what their anger looks like on a piece of paper. It might be a scribble, or it might look like a human or a monster. They might use one color or multiple colors. It's important not to make any comments about their drawing, but if they ask you about it, you can say something reflective like "So this is what your anger looks like" or "I see you used black to express your anger." Try not to analyze, interpret, judge, or shame their drawing for any reason. Even saying something like "Wow, I really like your drawing" is opinionated. This exercise helps your child externalize their anger, so instead of it living inside of them and controlling them, it's now on the outside looking in. It's not attached to them, and this will help them feel like they can control the anger instead. When they are done drawing, they can throw the paper away or hang it up. Most children will keep it as a reminder that they are in control, keeping it where they can see it, touch it, acknowledge it, and then walk away from it. And when they use their anger name or code word in the future, you will know how to help them by leaving an overstimulated or overwhelming environment or reminding them to use their positive coping skills.

Feed the Anger Box

I often transform an empty tissue box into an "anger box" with my young clients. This is a popular therapeutic intervention, and recently I even tried it at home with my own children. Anger boxes are great for little humans who have big feelings. Start by getting an empty tissue box and having your child decorate it with any craft material you have around the house, including pom-poms, glitter glue, stickers, or markers. Once the decorating part is done, explain to your child that they should write down anything that is angering them (or they can draw a picture), then place the paper in the box. This helps them visualize and externalize the problem and release it from inside. Sometimes children make the top of the box into a face with googly eyes and use the hole of the box as the mouth so they can "feed" their anger to the angry monster. If they draw or write something that seems urgent to you or is a safety matter, such as chronic severe bullying or suicidal ideation, you can immediately intervene. If they are worried a friend doesn't like them, for example, you can then foster a conversation with them to offer support and guidance. You can also use this idea for other emotions, creating a "grief box," a "worry box," or any box your child might need.

Lock It Away in a Jar

Another technique that helps children regulate is physically putting their thoughts and emotions in a jar for safekeeping until they are regulated and can process that emotion or thought later. The child writes/colors their emotions on a piece of paper and puts them in the jar. The jar should have a lid to shut it tight so the emotions are tucked safety inside the jar and not inside the child's body. This is important since many children keep their emotions locked up inside their body instead of releasing them. This intervention helps alleviate explosive eruptions of their emotions.

Stress Relief Splatter Painting

If your child is dysregulated or angry, encourage them to engage in stress relief splatter painting. Splatter painting is very therapeutic and cathartic for children. It's a physical way for children to release anger, stress, and other challenging emotions. Splatter painting also develops and strengthens fine and gross motor skills, and it's a fun, play-based activity that promotes artistic expression, creativity, and imagination. Splatter painting also supports color therapy, otherwise known as chromotherapy, if you use blue and green hues to support their mental, emotional, and physical well-being.

Craft It Out

Have your child craft what is angering them. If it's a person, let them create that person out of popsicle sticks, yarn, and googly eyes, then allow them to have a conversation with their creation so they can tell that person why they are mad at them. This activity helps a child channel their anger in a healthy way and direct their anger to the person they are angry with instead of taking it out on anyone nearby.

Anger Balloons

Fill balloons with water or washable paint and throw them against an outside wall that can be washed afterward. This action is very therapeutic and cathartic, and also fun. Children can even write or draw on the balloon before it is filled for an additional release!

Play Superhero

Teach your child how to be a superhero whose superpower is self-control. Have them put on an invisible cape or a special outfit that makes them feel confident. When they wear that cape, they have a big responsibility—to stay calm and in control of their body. Almost every child can think of someone they look up to, whether it's a family member, a superhero, or a mentor of some kind, like a teacher or coach. Even if it's not a specific person, most children can picture what a superhero looks like and how powerful a super-hero cape is. Have your child put on a real or imaginary superhero cape (most children choose for their cape to be invisible) when they need the superpower of control. When they are feeling dysregulated, they can put on their cape, anywhere, anytime, and this action will help empower them and give them a sense of control over their emotions. This will help them feel regulated and calm, sometimes instantaneously.

Anger Body Scan

Have your child scan their body from head to toe and notice where they feel their anger manifesting inside of them. Do they feel tense in their head, jaw, stomach, or hands? Do they feel the urge to hit, kick, yell, or bite? If your child has a problem hitting when they are angry, teach them to put their hands in their pockets. If your child has a problem kicking when they are angry, teach them to stomp on the ground. Once you identify where your child is physiologically feeling their anger, you can find an alternative solution for them to express it in a healthy and effective way.

Think of other play-based ways you can support your child when they are angry. The beauty of play-based parenting is that there are endless ways to help your child during problematic moments by simply thinking outside the box.

Chapter 13

Managing Defiance and Adverse Behaviors

"Education begins the moment we see children as innately wise and capable beings. Only then can we play along in their world."

—Vince Gowmon

HAVE YOU EVER BEEN IN A SITUATION WHERE YOUR CHILD is doing something you don't find appropriate, so you ask them to stop, but they look you dead in the eye and deliberately do it anyway? That type of deliberate defiance gets a parent's blood boiling really quickly and takes a tremendous amount of self-control and valor to remain calm.

———

Action Step: Take a moment and think about how you would respond. Would you:

- Raise your voice, scold them, and even threaten them that if they don't stop this behavior they will be disciplined in some way?

OR

- Stay calm and ask five more times for them to stop in hopes they will eventually give in and magically stop?

OR

- Do you take them aside and firmly give them a choice to comply or not?

Indulge me for a moment. Have you ever thought of diffusing defiance with play? You are the parent and ultimately in control of the situation, and how you react will influence how your child responds.

Defiance can look like asserting power and control, or it can look like disrespect. Let's say your child sticks their tongue out at you.

Action Step: Take a moment and think about how you would respond. Would you:

- Take offense (how dare they) and scold them.

OR

- Choose to playfully stick your tongue out at them and make silly faces and movements with your hands so they learn that sticking their tongue out isn't a powerful way to be defiant.

The power in sticking out the tongue is dissipated by the playfulness. The teaching moment of learning the behavior expectation on how to respect adults comes later.

———

When you respond with playfulness, you quickly put out the fire, take an accelerated shortcut, and immediately "Pass Go." Play is the fast track to diffuse defiance. With play, you also alter the power dynamic and obtain a power boost to get ahead in the parenting game.

I know these moments aren't easy, especially if there is an audience present. Publicly scolding or punishing your child is not the most effective choice, even though your pride as a parent might be bruised in the moment. Public shaming is more about you attempting or appearing to be in control, especially in the eyes of others. When your child is being defiant, you need to put your pride aside. It is very important not to publicly embarrass or shame your child in front of others, especially peers. Don't embarrass or shame a misbehaving child in front of others to "teach them a lesson." Try to remember that this moment is not about you and it's not about the quality of your parenting. It's not about saving face. It's about teaching your child how to behave respectfully. This moment is about finding the underlying cause to their behavior and articulating to them that their conduct is not acceptable. It's about teaching them they can be upset, but they need to handle it differently.

When a child feels out of control or emotionally dysregulated, they often try to assert power, and the only way they know how to do that is to argue back with you no matter what the cost. It's your job to teach them that there is another way, peacefully. I suggest pulling them aside and quietly, calmly, and firmly telling them that you see they are upset, acknowledging and validating the emotion, and then let them know that the behavior they are displaying is not respectful or acceptable. The separation of behavior and emotion needs to be clearly distinguished. Then invite your child to tell you what's wrong. Allow them an opportunity to show you what's bothering them. They may not oblige because they are still seeking control and will purposely withhold that information to try to empower themselves. As frustrating as this is, trying to force that information out of them is more about the power struggle than it is diffusing the situation. Once they are regulated and calm, you can ask them what triggered them earlier that day. They might not even know what triggered them or may not be able to articulate it, so expecting them to know and pressuring them to tell you may just make the situation worse.

The first thing to do in this scenario is to stop whatever you are doing (unless you're driving, and then you can decide if you need to pull over) and be present with them. This may be frustrating because you might be in the middle of something important, but the more present and connected you are, the faster you will get positive results and better behavior. Then get on their level and look them in the eye. If you think they also need a gentle touch, that's fine. Let them know you're there for them, even if you are angry or frustrated with them. Validate their emotion and also be reflective of the behavior you are observing. Ask fewer questions and use more statements, which requires more communication with fewer commands, more compassion and fewer consequences, more nurturing and less yelling, and more connection and less control.

Once you are fully present with your child, give them a choice to continue the undesirable behavior and receive a predetermined consequence or stop the behavior and move on. Ask your child if they need processing time to think about their decision or if they need your help figuring out how to solve the problem. Once your child decides, be consistent and follow through. If they continue being defiantly disrespectful and you have a predetermined consequence, make sure it happens. Depending on the severity, you can assess whether your child can earn something back if their behavior quickly improves after the explosive moment. But with defiance specifically, this could be a loophole they start taking advantage of, so I would lessen the consequence rather than eliminate it completely.

On the flip side, if they comply and immediately stop the challenging behavior and you told them you are letting it go, follow through and move on. Don't keep bringing it up, hold a grudge, or use the incident against them. If their behavior starts to become a pattern, you can tell them you are observing repetition in their behavior, but don't say to them that they "always" misbehave in public because most of the time that isn't true. Instead of a light bulb going off in their head and them saying, "Yes, Mom, you are right," they will just hear that they are bad and wonder why they should behave at all if they "always" misbehave and get in trouble anyway.

Give your child a reason to change. Let them know you believe they can change. Stop focusing on the past and the problem, and start focusing on the present and the solution. Catch them in the moments they are complying and praise them for good behavior. They will begin to notice that they are getting positive attention for their positive behavior and will most likely repeat it because it feels good. No child likes getting in trouble, even the most troubled and defiant child, and every child deserves praise and fresh new chances. Empower your children by relinquishing some of your power. This alone will change a child's behavior despite how defiant they are.

Defiance is often a cry for connection, power, and control. Children do not get enough of these three things in everyday life. They are constantly being told what to do and how to do it. Even though there is an underlying hierarchy in a parent-child relationship, children still need some sense of empowerment and respect. If they don't, how else are they going to learn critical-thinking and problem-solving skills?

It takes a lot more energy to be defiant than compliant. I haven't met one child who wants to deliberately misbehave. Children don't act out solely to manipulate you. That's a myth. They typically act out because they don't feel connected or empowered. When a child is being defiant, the first things a parent should think about are how connected they are to their child, if they need to exercise ways to empower their child to make more choices, or whether they should validate their child's voice more often. But instead, the second a child becomes defiant, a parent typically will jump to anger and punish the child for acting out. They think, "How dare they!" instead of "How have I played a role in their behavior and what can I do to help them?" Remember, it's a child's job to test limits and push boundaries. It's how they learn and experiment with you and the world.

I was recently talking to a friend about his child's behavior. He said his child was being outwardly defiant and not listening at home or to her sports coach and some of her teachers at school. I know this child, and I didn't jump to something like Oppositional Defiant Disorder because I felt the problematic behavior was environmental and more of a cry for connection. I reminded the parent that this child's younger sibling just started at the same school, and his older child might have felt like some of the autonomy she felt at her school was gone. This child had been the only child from her family at this school for about four years. But then, all of a sudden, her little sibling shows up and she has to share the spotlight and attention. When they would walk in the hallways, the younger sibling would often get ample attention from the other students, which I'm sure the older sibling internalized. She may have started growing a little resentful even though she loves her little sister.

He asked for advice, so I suggested that he provide more opportunities for empowerment and autonomy as well as spend more one-on-one time with the older sibling to strengthen their connection. I also recommended that the parent give the older sibling a few more responsibilities and privileges. For example, he could give the older sibling a later bedtime than her younger sister, even if it was only ten minutes later, or let the older child go out and get the mail independently (depending on age and where the mailbox is located). The parent can watch from the sidewalk, but it's a special "older" privilege that a child can only do because they are of a certain age, which is somewhat of a rite of passage.

Later that week after we spoke, the parent acknowledged he never considered that the older sister would be affected by the younger sister attending the same school or that amping up empowerment and connection would minimize his daugher's defiance. He told me he took my advice and took his oldest daughter on a nighttime bike ride, which the child thought was special because it was only with her dad and it was nighttime.

Sometimes we forget the little things we can do to help facilitate connection and positive behavior. Sometimes it takes more than one nighttime bike ride, but never underestimate micro-connection moments with your child. This little girl didn't want to get in trouble for defiant behavior, and she certainly didn't have the motivation or desire to directly talk about why she was behaving this way to her parents. There was a subtle shift in enhancement of play, connection, and power, and the problem was solved. He also asked me how to empower his child and help her feel validated and in control. Here is what I shared with him.

Autonomy Through the Developmental Life Cycle

Young children have a natural desire for independence and control. Helping your child achieve a sense of autonomy is helpful for healthy development. Autonomy helps prepare children to feel safe and confident in the world and will help them learn how to make good decisions later on in life. Since so much of the world is out of a child's control, they will seek ways to have autonomy, with or without your guidance, and will go to any means possible to get it. It's much better to give your child autonomous opportunities than for them to take them defensively and defiantly.

According to Erik Erikson's stages of psychosocial development, the autonomy versus shame stage occurs between eighteen months and two to three years old. During this stage, toddlers and preschoolers are egocentric and hyper-focused on developing a greater sense of self-control. If this stage is stunted or skipped because they aren't given opportunities to be autonomous, these children may suffer from low self-image, a lack of confidence, and indecisiveness later on in life. In my professional opinion, defiant behavior could also arise because they are constantly seeking and fighting for autonomy, power, and control.

A young child desires autonomy because developmentally they want to feel competent, independent, and capable to make their own choices and master aspects of their life and the world they live in. According to Rogers and Sawyers (1988), "Children are curious and when they want to explore something new, play is the best way to master competence." Young children depend on their parents for almost everything, but if autonomy is denied, a child will rebel and feel a sense of panic because they have no control of the world they live in. This may lead to disrespectful or defiant behavior. But if parents learn how to empower their children, the family system will function in a positive, peaceful, and effective manner.

Self-Efficacy

One of my favorite psychologists, Dr. Albert Bandura, whom I was fortunate enough to meet at a conference years ago, coined the term *self-efficacy* and defined it as "people's beliefs in their capabilities to exercise control over their own functioning and over events that affect their lives" (1997). Therefore, one's sense of self-efficacy can provide the foundation for motivation, engagement, well-being, confidence, and personal accomplishment. A lack of self-efficacy can also be a risk factor for academic failure and substance abuse, which is why it's so important to start empowering and providing opportunities for autonomy while children are young.

Give Them Authority

One of the best ways to empower children is by giving them choices and a voice. When a parent trusts a child to make decisions, the child feels a sense of mastery and develops confidence. So what choices can you allow your child to make based on their age, cognitive level, and developmental level? A toddler or preschooler may get a sense of control and feel empowered by making choices about what shirt they are going to wear or making the choice between eating one of two preferred snacks at lunchtime. A school-aged child might be able to choose what is for dinner once a week or what movie the family watches for family movie night. Anytime you can give your child the opportunity to make a decision, it will help motivate them, engage them, and empower them.

Give Them Responsibility

It's important for children to feel a sense of belonging. If they know they are an active contributor in their home and their family, they tend to be more invested, engaged, and motivated to help with chores and other daily tasks. Responsibility can be taught as early as toddlerhood, and can further develop the older a child gets. So what can you let go of that your child can accomplish on their own? Maybe it's making their bed every morning or cleaning their dishes after a meal. Whatever it is, children need a sense of mastery to feel engaged and empowered. So make sure you allow opportunities for this to happen. They are capable of so much more than we imagine. If they offer to put the groceries away, let them, even if you can do it in half the time or they put things in the wrong spot. Let them pour the milk on their cereal even if they might spill it all over the counter. They learn by doing, and you will help them so much in the process.

Give Them Space

Where is the one place in your home that your child feels safe and a sense of control over? Most likely their sanctuary is their bedroom. A place they can go to be alone. A place where they can be who they want, however they want. A place they can take ownership over. This haven can also be a special place in the home where they have a bean bag, blankets, pillows, and other materials like a journal and art supplies. Each sibling in the home can choose their own space as long as it's preapproved or collaboratively created with a parent. This space is not intended to be a punitive space or a reward space. It's more like a free space. Once it's established, it's theirs to spend time in throughout the day before school, after school, or on breaks. If your child has trouble leaving their space to actively function and participate in everyday family activities, you can set up a visual or auditory timer to limit the time they can be there. Just make sure they get time there daily and they know in advance how much time they can spend there each day.

Give Them Time

One of the best gifts you can give your child is your time. Give them time to talk to you. Give them time to process with you. Give them time to vent. And give them time to share about their lives, their emotions, and their struggles. Having a conversation with your child doesn't necessarily mean you have to give them advice or share some life-changing knowledge, but more so an ear to listen to them. Listening and taking in what they are telling you is much more valuable than you sharing with them. These conversations are reserved just for them and should be focused solely on them. These types of conversations will build attachment, trust, safety, and a bridge to talk about tough topics the older they become.

Give Them Power

If your child is power seeking, provide an opportunity for them to play it out. Let them play teacher and you play student. Let them be the police and you be the bandit. Or let them be the parent and you be the child. Whatever the scenario, allow the child to lead with a sense of control in their play. This is just temporary, and it's just fantasy play, so if they want to be the doctor that gives you a shot or the pirate that ties you up with rope or makes you walk the plank, don't worry! Remember that they rarely get control in their lives, and this play is one way they get to feel empowered.

Strategic Play-Based Defiance

Let's talk about how to diminish defiance by using play-based techniques. When a child is acting defiantly, I am sure the last thing most parents think of is to defuse the situation through play. Some parents might argue that they are rewarding the challenging behavior. I disagree. A parent doesn't always have to win a power struggle just because they are the adult. Adults make mistakes all the time. So why not put the fire out with play? This shift in dynamic may change your child's behavior the first time instead of butting heads and engaging in power struggles time after time. When you play, you are choosing to connect and engage with your child; when you power struggle you are choosing to disengage with your child. Arguing and fighting for power loses the connection between the two of you, but playing will help connect you. Let's talk about some ways to achieve this.

Defiance Dance Party

The last thing your child will expect when they are acting defiantly is a dance party. In graduate school, I attended a couples therapy conference, and the speaker taught us about a strategic therapy technique where, in the middle of an argument with your spouse, you leave the room and come back naked. Most times when couples did this, the abruptness and shock changed the overall vibe in the room and they ended up laughing, breaking up the fight, and moving on a little more calmly together. And as crazy as it sounds, that shift in momentum is the point. A similar strategy—not the naked part, but the stop-them-in-their tracks part—will work with your child. It will throw them off when they least expect it, undo their defiance, and change the power struggle altogether.

———————

Action Step: What do you think would happen mid-argument if you said to your child, "This conversation is very important to both of us, but let's pause for a moment and listen to some music, have an impromptu dance party, or take a walk to cool off. Then we can come back to talking."

———————

I guarantee when you pause for a break and come back, both of you will be calmer and may even see things differently than if you kept arguing in the heat of the moment. This way, you can both walk or dance out some of the emotional frustration through music and movement without taking it out on each other.

Schedule a Family Meeting

If you notice arguments with your child becoming more frequent, schedule a time to argue or talk about the problem. You can schedule it in the moment when an issue arises or hold a scheduled weekly meeting about anything and everything that is bothering your child (or you). The goal for these meetings is not to store up all of the "bad" moments throughout the week and then spend twenty minutes shaming, criticizing, and condemning each other. This time is used wisely to express issues constructively and come up with changes and solutions to what isn't working within the family system and household. The child may not be capable of doing this, but as the parent, it's important to not only look at their behaviors but look at your own as well. It's also important to talk about what is working and what isn't working. Make sure you sandwich the feedback: starting with a positive, adding the negative, and ending with a positive.

How to Use Play to Help Your Children Do Unpreferred Activities

One complaint I often get from parents is that their children procrastinate or defy them when they are asked to do chores, homework, or anything else that isn't a preferred activity. Most often, children aren't trying to be outwardly defiant, they just aren't motivated to do the mundane task you are asking. But don't fret! I have a plethora of play-based ideas on how to get your children to be less defiant toward unpreferred requests. A parent can make almost every activity fun. In Chapter 1, we talked about play-based ways to get your children to clean the stairs or their room, two very common scenarios for many families. Here are some additional ideas for some other common activities.

Making the Bed

When a child is having difficulty making their bed in the morning, a parent can turn it into a game by timing their child and challenging them to get it done faster each day. This competitive type of play can help parents get things done in a play-based way. Set a timer to see how quickly they can make their bed—and have them try to break their record each day. You can even keep a visual progress chart in their room to track their times. Children think this is such a fun game and get competitive with themselves. And while they work on their motor skills, you get a clean bed each morning!

Playful Homework Brain Breaks

When my children aren't in the mood for homework, we play games in between problems if they are working on math, in between words if they are working on spelling, or in between sentences if they are doing a writing assignment. Similarly, after each problem, word, or sentence, you can take micro brain breaks and have your child run around the kitchen island or retrieve something in the house—like a mini scavenger hunt. You can also mix it up and have them do various activities during their breaks, like doing jumping jacks or taking a sip of water. This may seem like a lot of extra work, but think about how much time and energy you'll be saving from the standoffs, tears, and power struggles you typically have with your child that drag out the homework process for hours.

General Chores

Anytime you can make chores into a game or a competition, you will get more compliance from your child. Come up with a variety of games your child can play to determine what chores they will complete that week. For example, get some plastic cups and a small ping-pong ball. Write different chores on pieces of paper and tape one inside each cup. One cup can say "take out trash," while other cups can have chores like "feed the pet," "clean the dishes," "set the table," or "make your bed." The chores will depend on your child's age, development, and skill level. Set up the cups in a straight line. Each member of the family (parents included) tries to throw the ball into one of the cups. Whatever cup the ball lands in determines what chore they are doing for the week. Mixing up chore responsibilities each week also helps keep tasks exciting and fresh instead of feeling stuck doing the same job week after week. One of the cups could even have a "free chore week" note, meaning that person doesn't have to do any chores that week. Another way to make chores more fun is by playing hopscotch dunk. Set up a hopscotch game using a play carpet, chalk, or tape. Then throw a beanbag, and whatever square the beanbag lands in, that is the chore you're assigned. Lastly, you can get a game wheel and write different chores on each section of the wheel. Have your child spin the wheel, and wherever the wheel stops is what chore your child will have.

Leaving the House Quickly

If a child is having trouble getting ready for school on time, have a dinosaur puppet "chase" them until they are dressed and ready so they don't get bitten by the dinosaur. You can also use colorful sensory stones to play the floor is lava to get your children to leave the house quickly. Set up the colorful stones across the floor and have your child walk on them to leave the house. The goal is to leave the house as quickly as possible, so make it sound urgent by getting into the game. If you do not want to purchase sensory stones, use colorful pieces of construction paper taped to the floor or make it imaginary. You can also play the exploding volcano game, where you and your children imagine a volcano inside the home is about to erupt, so everyone has to move quickly out the front door. Or you can even pretend your front door is a portal that transports them anywhere their imagination will take them.

Putting on Sunscreen

Putting on sunscreen is important for every child, but it is often an unpreferred activity, especially if the sunscreen is being applied to their face. Many children don't like the feel or smell of sunscreen, and they also don't want to stop what they are doing to put it on, especially if they are already at their preferred location like the pool, beach, or park. If you can, I recommend putting on sunscreen before you leave for your desired location to lessen the power struggle. But if you've already arrived, instead of arguing with your child, trying to teach them the benefits of wearing sunscreen, or guilting them into wearing it, make it play-based and fun. I suggest having them pretend they are at a carnival and you are painting their face in whatever imaginary colors or styles they can imagine. It's best if they close their eyes while you put the sunscreen on their face, describing the colors you are pretending to use and what their face looks like throughout the process.

Brushing Teeth

I often hear that parents struggle with getting their children to brush their teeth. If you make brushing teeth fun and playful, it will become much more of an enjoyable experience rather than a dreadful one. Put on some music for two minutes and have your children dance while they brush. Or put fun jokes on sticky notes and post them all over the bathroom mirror so they will have a fun distraction while they brush. If your children can't read yet, you can exchange the jokes for fun cartoon drawings instead.

With just these few examples, you can easily understand how to make many less-preferred tasks into play-based activities. What activities can you make playful now that you know how?

Chapter 14

Playing with Food for Picky Eating

"It is a happy talent to know how to play."

—RALPH WALDO EMERSON

ONE OF THE BIGGEST CHALLENGES PARENTS TELL ME THEY have with their children is getting them to try new and less-preferred foods. It is such a prominent parenting concern I am excited to share my quick and effective tips on how to make mealtime playful and fun so your children will eat—especially those veggies. Parents have enough on their plate (no pun intended) and so many other things to worry about besides struggling with their child during mealtime.

Benefits of Playing with Food

The main benefit of having children play with food is to make mealtime more colorful, playful, and fun. It will also help minimize anxiety and power struggles around food and mealtime. Playing with food and making mealtime fun will allow parents and children to spend more time cultivating a connection with one another during mealtime rather than spending the time in tears and arguments.

Connection Cooking

One of the most prominent places I have seen parents and children grow closer is in the kitchen. Preparing a meal and cooking together can be very intimate and therapeutic, and sharing this experience has many mental, social, and emotional benefits. Plus, cooking together stimulates tactile functioning through the numerous sensory receptors in our hands that we use to prepare a meal. Tactile stimulation is essential for children's brain and neurological development, as well as establishing secure attachments. Tactile stimulation also alleviates stress symptoms, improves the development of the nervous system, decreases heart rate, increases circulation, releases the anti-stress hormone oxytocin, and improves the immune system.

And when you and your child cook together, you are communicating, connecting, and playing. This enhanced relationship and experience can improve a child's willingness to try new foods. When you cook with your child, you are activating your entire sensory system by using your senses of sight, smell, taste, touch, and hearing to create something delicious while you are talking and listening to one another, working as a team.

Activating the Sensory System

Children love to experiment with food. When they are young, they are often seeing, smelling, touching, and tasting many foods for the first time. Indeed, trying new food is all about our senses, and there are effective strategies for how to use a child's sensory system to encourage them to try new foods. Utilizing a child's sensory system enables them to "play" with their food by using their senses to experiment with new and less-preferred foods. For example, the first time your child is exposed to a new or less-preferred food, the goal isn't to have them eat it but to play with it. They can expose themselves to the smell, texture, and maybe even the taste of the food by licking it, squishing it, throwing it, and playing with it. Eventually, after multiple exposures, a child will most likely take a bite. They may not like the food after taking a bite, but the goal is to have them try it.

If you have a child who prefers the texture of crunchy food, try adding granola to their yogurt or chips on their sandwich, or put yogurt in a sensory pop-it and freeze it. If they prefer soft foods, experiment with smoothies, purees, and soups. If your child doesn't like cooked broccoli, try it raw. If they don't like the texture of avocado, try eating it as guacamole, or try tomatoes as salsa! Foods can be eaten in all sorts of ways with differing textures—sometimes it just takes a little experimentation and creativity with the preparation and presentation!

Using Exposure Therapy to Try New Foods

Who says a child has to be forced to eat a bunch of foods they don't like? Children learn at varying paces, and parents should be meeting their child where they are, uniquely. That means not comparing them to their siblings or peers, or forcing them to eat something in a timely matter or be threatened by a consequence. Each child is different, and some may like certain foods while others don't. Having a growth mindset to eating is vital to mealtime success.

Research has suggested that it can take anywhere from twelve to twenty-four times for a child to be exposed to a new food before they will try it. I remember how much I hated salad, brussels sprouts, and asparagus when I was a child. And now I love them all. Sometimes it takes years to sophisticate our palates. Food aversions are common for children. If your child is eating nutritious meals most of the time and adding new foods to their diet on a regular basis, pat yourself on the back—you're doing a good job. The key is to expose them to food a little at a time, without force. When you force a child to eat foods they don't want to, you are doing yourself a disservice because most likely the outcome will not only be more stubbornness and defiance but also a severed relationship between you and your child. On the other hand, if you are enabling your child and they are only eating a handful of the same foods over and over again or eating an abundance of sugary, processed food, you have some work to do. Exposing your child to a variety of foods at a young age will help encourage them to try new foods. Young children also learn best by role-modeling, so when you eat the new food with them, they are more likely to try it, too. Remember the connection piece when you eat food together.

To slowly expose your child to new foods, start by following these steps:

1. Show your child a photo of the food you want them to learn more about. Name the food and describe to them what it smells, feels, and tastes like. Also, ask them what they notice about the food and have them describe what they see and what they assume it will taste like. Will it be sweet or sour? Will it be soft or crunchy?

2. See if there is a play food of that same item. Let them get familiar with seeing it, naming it, and playing with it. Then go to the store with your child and show them the real food in the store. Ask them to look, touch, and smell it as well as describe their initial observations. Was their hypothesis correct? Ask them if they are ready to try it, but don't force it. If they aren't, put it back on the shelf and try again the next time you are at the store. Once they are ready, buy the food and bring it home. Maybe the store clerk can even put that food in a special bag for your child to carry home.

3. Once you are home, have your child put the food in a special place on the counter or in the fridge. If your child picked a cantaloupe, cut it open and show them what the fruit looks like inside. They can explore the shape, color, smell, and texture of the fruit. If they want to smell it or lick it, that's fantastic. If they just want to play with it or squeeze it between their fingers, that is acceptable, too. You may even get lucky and they'll take a bite! Praise them for any progress they make with the food, especially if they taste it!

Since it may take your child a dozen or more times to be exposed to a new food before they will actually take a bite, remember to celebrate the small wins along the way. You can even try offering a positive reinforcement (sticker, mini marshmallow, chocolate chip) each time they try a new food or a less-preferred food. Some parents aren't fond of this method, but it worked magic with my children—they eat basically any vegetable or new food I give them, not only because of the positive reinforcement but because they trust me and the connection we have built.

How to Play with Food

Playing with food is encouraged, if not necessary, for a young child to eat. Children learn best through meaningful playful experiences. By playing with their food, they are able to explore and experiment with their senses, learn how to trust food, and determine what they like and what they don't like. Maybe playing with their food looks like them making a design with the food on their plate, or maybe it means they dissect it and deconstruct it. If your child wants to touch the food with their hands instead of a utensil, go with it. This means they are still wanting to try the food, just not in an adult-like traditional way. Or maybe instead of their hands, you can make it fun by giving them tongs to pick up their food with instead of a fork or spoon. This is the time to really think like a child!

Here are some of my practical, easy-to-implement, play-based ways to help your child try new foods:

Choo Choo Train

Have you ever been to a revolving sushi restaurant where you can choose your food from a conveyor belt? This intervention is a similar concept. First, assemble an electric toy train and put it on your countertop, table, or floor. Next, prepare food for your child. Although you won't be able to put some items on the train (for example, spaghetti or soup), you can offer a variety of foods for your child to try in a fun, creative, and playful way. As the train goes around and around, your child can playfully pick up one of the items on the train to try.

Dump Truck

For this strategy, get a toy dump truck and fill the back with whatever food you want your child to try. Your child can push the dump truck around on the counter or the floor as they try the food from the back. The dump truck can act as the "plate," or you can push it back and forth on the floor or table and take turns eating from it.

Family Style

Have you ever served a meal with no plates? Put down a clean, washable tablecloth on your table. I suggest getting an inexpensive disposable one to throw away as soon as the meal is done. Pour the meal on the table with no plates (utensils optional). Children will think this is so fun, they are more likely to eat the food on the table. Go big and serve spaghetti with a variety of vegetables, such as broccoli and mushrooms. Don't forget the Parmesan cheese to sprinkle on top!

Cookie Cutters

Use cookie cutters to prepare your child's food. There are so many options these days, with cookie cutters shaped like animals, letters, numbers, hearts, etc. Bring a few out and ask your child which one they want, then cut their sandwich into that shape or animal!

Score the Food Taste-Test Game

Children love playing games, so why not make mealtime more fun? For this strategy, get a piece of paper and cut it into ten pieces. Number the pieces from one to ten. Place the pieces of paper next to your children. Then one by one, serve your child a variety of new and less-preferred foods. Once your child sees, smells, touches, or even tastes the food, have your child rate that food on a scale from one to ten, using their score sheets (a.k.a. their pieces of paper), just like a judge at a competition. Since it's a fun game and not a forced meal, they are more apt to try the new or less-preferred foods.

Ice Cube Tray

A mistake I often see parents make is serving portion sizes that are too big for children. This results in the child being overwhelmed and refusing to eat, which further causes power struggles, anxiety, and negative feelings around food and mealtime. So consider serving your child's meal in an ice cube tray. Ice cube trays provide small squares to help parents with portion control. Children can always ask for more but struggle to ask for less. Pair preferred foods with less-preferred foods in the different compartments on the tray. The ice cube compartments should have a variety of foods with varying colors, smells, and textures. You could put something crunchy (pretzels, raw apples, cucumbers, or carrots) next to something creamy (hummus, yogurt, or sun butter), and something soft (banana or avocado) alongside a protein of choice (pepperoni, salami, or beef sticks) in the other compartments.

Making Mealtime Fun

Try to be consistent. Plan to have meals at the same time each day and make mealtime something they look forward to throughout the day. Think of things to do that are only done during mealtime, like playing a special game (Would You Rather, I Spy, or a staring contest) or putting white paper down as a tablecloth with some crayons and letting them take color breaks throughout their meals. Children eat slowly, so do not rush them. And if you are willing and able, have a dance party to get out some wiggles throughout the meal so they aren't expected to stay seated at a table for a long time.

Give Children Agency

When children feel like they have a say and some control over a situation, they are more likely to cooperate. Start a meal by having them pick which cup and plate they want for mealtime so they have some authority, considering they probably don't have much control over the meal they are going to eat. Or have your child be part of the process of shopping with you and picking out something new to try to give them a sense of belonging, empowerment, and ownership. You can also invite your child to cook the food in the kitchen with you. This investment into the foods they pick and prepare will help them want to try new foods. Maybe your child can even create the family menu once a week.

Encouraging Playing with Food

Have you ever watched the movie *A Christmas Story* from 1983? If so, do you remember the scene where the mom in the movie helps her youngest son eat by saying, "Show me how the piggies eat"? The child proceeds to "eat" his dinner by diving into his plate headfirst and eating with his mouth instead of utensils.

The scene begins with the narrator of the film, the oldest brother, saying, "Every family has a kid who won't eat. My kid brother had not eaten voluntarily in over three years." Visually, you see the younger brother playing with his food by stacking mashed potatoes on his fork and picking up small pieces of food before throwing them back onto his plate. The mom's first response to his behavior is, "Don't play with your food, eat it!" The dad quickly then chimes in by saying, "You stop playing with your food or I'll give you something to cry about!"

But then there's a switch. This is the switch I talk about in this book. The mom uses a play-based parenting technique to help her child eat. Once she does, the child stops moping and moaning, and they start connecting and laughing together, making mealtime more fun and less threatening. She makes mealtime playful and engaging, and it works! Maybe I was destined to be a play therapist because I have adored that scene since I was a little girl. It's a play-based parenting technique from more than forty years ago that stands the test of time. The biggest barrier to children playing with their food is the parents. Can you imagine this scene taking place in a busy restaurant? I believe most parents would be mortified if their child started snorting and eating headfirst in front of others. I get it. I might feel that way, too. But there is no reason a child can't explore food during mealtime in a play-based, tactile, sensory-driven way at home. Will they make a mess? Probably. Messes can be cleaned up. I believe a mess is easier to handle than a power struggle. Parenting is about picking your battles, and if I can help my child develop a positive relationship with me and food, I am willing to try just about anything. I'm not saying parents shouldn't have behavioral expectations for mealtime and that it should be a free-for-all. I'm just saying mealtime doesn't have to be so rigid, especially when children are young. Play-based parenting is all about being flexible, fluid, and fun. There will be time to teach them table manners as they grow.

What to Avoid

I urge you not to prepare your children separate meals from the ones the entire family is eating simply because they are "picky." This only enables the child, which will create more problems long term. Nor should you avoid reintroducing less-preferred foods because you've tried a few times with no luck. This also means that you don't offer a replacement meal if they refuse your initial meal. They are not being punished by you refusing to make them another meal; it is simply a boundary and limit you have placed. If they don't want to eat the meal you made, that is ultimately their choice, and it's also your choice not to make a replacement meal.

Children can become "picky" when they are offered the same preferred foods all the time. As I mentioned before, if they don't eat a food one way, think of a way to prepare and present that food again differently. And if a parent enables their child by providing the same food over and over again and only offering a lot of sugary, processed foods, their child's bodies will start craving the sugar and carbs, and nothing else will compare. Try limiting those types of foods as much as you can, and continue to expose and encourage your child to try new and healthier food options often.

Research has shown that nutrition affects a child's mood and behavior, so make sure you limit sugar, processed foods, and synthetic dyes. These have been linked to undesirable behaviors and worsening behavioral symptoms, so why would you want to contribute to that? Also, as I mentioned before, try not to force your child to eat new foods, raise your voice, or shame them for not wanting to try it. Avoid using any threatening language or punishing them if they don't eat what's on their plate.

PART IV

How to Get Your Children to Behave

Chapter 15

Achieving Better Listening and Cooperation

"When we treat children's play as seriously as it deserves, we are helping them feel the joy that's to be found in the creative spirit. It's the things we play with and the people who help us play that make a great difference in our lives."

—FRED ROGERS

HOW MANY TIMES HAVE YOU GOTTEN FRUSTRATED BECAUSE your child won't listen to you or follow directions? Honestly, if you said a number close to 1,374,789,062 in your head, that is probably accurate. Young children tend to be in an egocentric part of their lives and don't have the cognitive capacity to listen and follow directions like adults do. Young children also have low attention spans and high levels of emotionality.

Some children have a more people-pleasing, compliant personality and temperament, but there is not one child living and breathing in the world who listens and cooperates 100 percent of the time. And when your children do listen, let me ask you this: Is it because you threaten to punish them and take something away, or is it because you bribe or beg them with an incentive to comply? I believe in positive reinforcement when given correctly, but those two strategies, which may appear to work in the short term, aren't an effective long-term parenting strategy. Both will have ramifications if done chronically and will have unpleasant side effects if used often.

This chapter will explain five simple steps to get children to listen and cooperate with a parent's requests. In my own experience, most children will comply after this five-step process, but if they do not, the parent sets a boundary or gives a predetermined consequence if the undesired behavior persists. This way the child knows from the get-go what could happen if they choose to engage in undesirable behavior, and the responsibility is on the child, not the parent. By setting up the "choice," the child also feels like they are empowered and have a sense of control.

Let's dig a little deeper into these five steps.

1. Use an attention request: Attention requests can be verbal, auditory, or visual. You can use regular household items, such as a kitchen timer, a bell, chimes, or musical instruments, or simply sing a song or engage in a clapping sequence. Teach your child what the attention request is and what it means. Then every time your child hears or sees this request, they know to stop and listen to you.

2. Gain eye contact: If you don't have eye contact, your child is most likely not listening, so get down on their level or pick them up so you are eye to eye before giving them an instruction. The exception to this is for a neurodivergent child who cannot or is uncomfortable making eye contact.

3. Give a compliance command: A compliance command is a short and concise request for desirable behavior. The command is not a question but a statement. "Can you please take out the trash?" is not as effective as "I need you to take out the trash." Give only one instruction at a time so your child doesn't feel flooded, forget, or get distracted. If they are in the middle of a preferred task, don't rush them or expect them to immediately stop and do what you want. Give them a moment or two to process your request and transition.

4. Give the child a choice to comply or receive a consequence:
If you tried to make your request a play-based one and your child
is still refusing to follow instruction, remind your child of the rules
and what the consequence will be if they do not cooperate.

5. Praise or consequence: If the child cooperates, immediately give
them a high five or a hug and tell them you are proud of them for
making a good choice. You can also give them a raffle ticket, a sticker,
or a good behavior ticket for an incentive. Remember, incentives
don't have to cost money. Children love extra computer time or
staying up past their bedtime. If the child doesn't cooperate, stay
calm and immediately give them their predetermined consequence.
Be sure to see it through.

Children ultimately have the desire to do the right thing and
want to please their caregivers. They flourish in a positive, supportive, and encouraging environment. They also thrive on acceptance,
love, and approval. Children will learn to listen and comply with
your requests when they are directly taught, reminded, and given
clear boundaries for acceptable and unacceptable behavior. They are
also more likely to listen and cooperate if they feel positively connected to you and can accomplish the request in a playful way.

Here are some play-based ways to get your child to listen and
cooperate:

Play Ninja

Teach your child how to be a ninja and be as stealth and quiet as
possible when you need them to listen. You can walk around the
house with them, tiptoeing as you tell them what they need to do,
whether it's get dressed, brush their teeth, or wash their hands for
mealtime. Children will stop what they are doing to play and will
typically comply quickly because washing hands like a ninja is much

more fun than washing them because they are dirty and their mom or dad told them to.

Robot Requests

When you want your child to listen and comply, turn into a robot and give your request in a robotic voice while using robotic movements. Your child is more likely to listen and engage when you make the request fun and playful.

The Puppet Told Me To

Similar to the robot request, use a puppet to ask your child to throw something away or get a task done. This way, the request comes from the cute, friendly, and trusted puppet and not the parent. The child may be more compliant if they hear the request from their favorite puppet instead of their mom or dad. Don't have a puppet? Use a sock, paper bag, oven mitt, or even your hand!

Make Your Child the Boss

Empower your child to become the boss and have them make a request to get something done by asking their stuffed animal or doll to listen and cooperate. The child will obviously have to help their chosen assistant, but the task will get done because the child will be empowered and in control. And they "get out" of doing the task because in their mind and through their play, their chosen assistant is doing all the work.

The Silent and Still Game

Play the Silent and Still Game when you need your children to listen and cooperate. This isn't necessarily a new concept, but it's an effective one. Anytime you turn a request into a game, children will become intrigued and more engaged. Ask your child to be silent and still for thirty seconds and time them. You may need to practice making sure they can accomplish this in the allotted time. Then increase the time increment a few times to challenge them to see the longest they can go without making a noise or moving their body. You can even play with them because they might be invested if they know they can "beat" you in the game. Once you play a few times and know their capacity for being silent and still, give your request when you have their full attention and when your child will be calm and ready to receive an instruction.

Sing a Song

I taught university-level courses with adults for almost a decade and often needed to get my students' attention quickly. They may have thought I was a little nutty, but when I needed their attention, I would start singing a song. The one I liked best was "If You're Happy and You Know It" because it's interactive and they have to clap or stomp when you ask them to participate. By the end of the first verse, I not only had everyone's attention but they were engaged and moving and singing playfully on command. And that was with adults; imagine how well this intervention works with children!

Turn Your Listening Ears On

This intervention is pretty straightforward, but when you need your child to listen, ask them to turn their listening ears on before you give your request for cooperation. Children can physically pretend to turn their ears on, or they may want you to do it for them. Playfully ask them for a sound check so you know their ears are on before you begin.

Show Me Six

An evidence-based behavior modification method advises parents to say "show me six" when a child is in the middle of a problematic behavior to prompt the child to stop and listen. You first have to teach them this auditory prompt and what the six prompts mean, but it works wonders to get children to stop and listen. The six behavior prompts are: hands on lap, listening ears on, mouth quiet, eyes on adult, body still, and feet on the ground. Once your child knows these six prompts, when you say "show me six," they should immediately freeze, do these six things immediately and simultaneously, and be prepared to listen to you.

These methods take some front-loading and some consistent teaching, but once they are learned and practiced, they will become second nature and work wonders for better listening, following directions, and better behavior.

Chapter 16

Enforcing Boundaries and Healthy Limits

"At the end of the day, the most overwhelming key to a child's success is the positive involvement of parents."

—Jane D. Hull

THIS CHAPTER WILL EXPLAIN HOW TO POSITIVELY IMPLEMENT healthy limits and enforce boundaries effectively. When life is predictable, a child is able to understand and make sense of it, which will help them behave more positively. When life is ambiguous and uncertain, children tend to go into a fight-or-flight mode and either disengage or become hypervigilant and overreactive. That's where establishing limits comes in. The purpose is not to punish but to set structure for your child, provide a consistent and predictable environment, and create a sense of safety. And yes, I'm glad you asked, setting limits can be done in a play-based way.

In grad school, I learned of a play therapy limit-setting intervention called the A.C.T Method, created by Garry Landreth, the founder of the Center for Play Therapy at the University of North Texas. As a play therapist, I have looked up to him for years. He is a play therapy guru, and I have so much respect for him and how he conducts child-centered play therapy. He is a natural and makes it look so effortless, although I know from experience that it's not as easy as it looks. Being a play therapist takes a certain kind of talent and doesn't come naturally for everyone. That's one of the reasons I wanted to write this book and help make a play-based parenting style more common and user-friendly for the everyday parent.

The A-C-T Method is a positive discipline strategy that encourages children to feel however they feel but not behave in any way they want to act. This is the basic concept of the A-C-T Method:

- Acknowledge a child's needs, wants, and emotions
- Communicate the limit
- Target acceptable and alternative actions, behaviors, and choices

Here is an example scenario:

- **A:** It appears like you are trying to hit your sister because she took your toy, and it seems like that made you angry. It's OK to be angry. When someone takes our toys without asking, it hurts our feelings.
- **C:** It's my job to keep you and your sister safe. And your sister is not for hitting. It's not safe or kind to hit another person, even if they made you angry and you are upset.
- **T:** We need to use our safe hands, so you can use this pillow to hit when you're mad.

During my play therapy classes in grad school, there were two differing perspectives when it came to setting limits with children. One perspective believed that limits should be set from the get-go and taught to children before any given situation. The other perspective believed that limits should be set on a case-by-case basis, depending on what was currently happening. I'll let you decide what is best for you and your child, but the point is that limits need to be set, whether you do it in advance or after a situation arises. My personal philosophy is that you need both: limits in advance to prevent disruptive behaviors and also situational limit setting when problematic behaviors occur. And always remember to show empathy with your expectations.

Creating Limits in the Home

In advance, think about the behavior expectations you have for your child. What general rules do you have in your home? When limit setting, teach your child what the limit looks like and repeat when needed. Show them examples of how they can express themselves more effectively in the future. Don't assume they already know; teach them how to behave the way you want them to. If you want them to use an indoor voice, show them what that looks like by giving examples based on your own voice levels. Shout and whisper, then ask your child if either of those are examples of an indoor voice. This teaching style will make it more fun to learn. They will probably laugh and say no, then give you the in-between voice that is an acceptable indoor voice. Practice and repeat with your child when needed until they no longer need a reminder.

How to Implement Limits

When your child is not making a safe choice, state the limit calmly and firmly. "When you hit other children on the playground it isn't safe, so we will have to leave." When you are setting limits, take the emotion out of it. Avoid saying something like, "It really hurts my feelings when you hit me" or "It makes Mommy sad when you draw on the walls." Instead, say, "The rule in our home is that we do not hit others when we are angry. When you are angry, you can hit the pillow or punching bag" or "We do not draw on the walls. Instead, you can draw on paper."

Limit Setting vs. Encouragement

A parent should not enable a child's disruptive behaviors just so they can avoid setting boundaries and limits with them. I have met parents who seem oblivious to their child's challenging behavior and parents who deny, defend, and minimize their child's problematic behavior. They know it's there but can't come to terms with it or can't effectively control it.

I was recently at the grocery store and saw a mom arguing with her child about something the girl wanted. The mom was saying no. Typical situation, right? The child started squirming in the cart and raising her voice at her mom, but the mom kept her cool and calmly said no over and over. Setting a boundary was important here, but let's dive deeper. The child escalated her behavior and began to swing at the mom, trying to hit her face and pull her hair. The mom continued to remain firm and calm with her boundary, not giving into the child's request. She gently replied instead with "Don't do that," but she was lacking the limit. I could tell the mom was embarrassed and frustrated, and as they turned the corner into the next aisle, I heard the child still yelling at the mom as her behaviors continued.

As much as I teach parents to stay calm in these moments, there is such a thing as being too calm. This mom was being bulldozed by her child and didn't do much about it except repeat "No, don't do that," over and over. In addition to her gentle reminder, I would have loved her to acknowledge the child's emotion and behavior, and be very specific about how the child could be handing their big feelings in a more positive or effective way. I would have loved for her to calmly set a limit and say, "I know you are upset and frustrated [or angry if they are super young] that I won't buy you cookies, but we do not yell in the store and we do not hit other people. That's not safe or respectful." Then she could have said something like "I need to get what's on my list. I'd like for you to show me what it's like to be behave in the store. You can be mad and also not yell and hit. If you can show me this, we can go to the park this afternoon or watch your favorite show when we get home. If not, then we won't be able to have any dessert after dinner and you'll miss out on going to the park today."

I see gentle-minded parents allow their child to express themselves however they please without any limits, boundaries, teaching moments, or consequences. They get hit over and over like a punching bag, and they just tolerate it so the child can freely express themselves. They don't use a firm voice, either, but that is just as unhealthy as the parent who yells at their child for misbehaving and then slaps on a punishment. Both are extreme ends of the spectrum, but my methods fit somewhere effectively in between.

I also believe that a parent should not force a child to do something by just saying "Because I said so" or without explaining "the why." You may know you are trying to get them to do something that isn't scary, but they don't know that. You may think something isn't a big deal, but they might. You may want to tell your child that everything is going to be fine, and maybe you're right, but invalidating their apprehension and fear around a specific situation is only a detriment to your relationship and their trust in you. You also want to be careful you don't limit them by letting them out of every request because of their anxiety; otherwise, they won't learn how to try new things and how to adapt to new situations. Instead, slowly and mindfully play out the situation that is holding your child back.

A few years ago, my son was taking swim classes. One day, I witnessed a child in his class refuse to get into the water. The child looked terrified, and I witnessed the parent and the swim instructor try to coerce the child into the water. The child was using all of their might to stay out of the water, and tensions were getting high. The parent and swim instructor were getting frustrated, and they both knew that this situation was holding up the class. After a few more minutes of tantrums and power struggles, the parent pulled the child away from the pool and told them they didn't have to participate in class that day. The second the fight was over, the child immediately stopped the disruptive behaviors and sat happily on the side of the pool. The parent had another child in a different class, so they ended up sitting next to me on a bench by the side of the pool until class was over.

As a rule, I typically don't give unsolicited advice. When a parent gives another parent unsolicited advice, it can feel very invalidating and shaming. We may mean well and be coming from a place of concern and support, but it also can feel critical and condescending to the parent receiving the feedback. That parent may feel like they aren't a good parent when they are trying their best, and they may feel weak, guilty, embarrassed, or ashamed before we even start speaking to them. When we give our unsolicited advice, it's like salt on a wound. As a parent giving the advice, we don't know the entire story, so we should always lead with kindness. That being said, after class, an opportunity opened up for me and I took it.

As we were packing up and drying off our children after class, the mom turned in my direction and said something along the lines of, "What a day, am I right?" I had so many ideas I wanted to share with her, but I didn't want to come across as better than her or a know-it-all. She didn't know what I did for a living, so I wanted to be a relatable mom, not an expert mom. I gave empathy and said, "Yes, I can relate. I have had those days before." I proceeded to tell her that I had struggled with getting my son to participate in coach-led classes before and offered to share some things that worked if she wanted. Then I left it open for her to respond one way or another. If she said no, I would have respected that and walked away. Luckily, she was open to my advice because she was at her wit's end arguing with her son each time they came to swim class.

I gently suggested some play-based ways to get him engaged at home; wearing goggles and searching for toys in the bath, buying a fun and colorful kickboard to play with in the pool, and suggesting he teach his toys how to swim in the bath as the swim coach to feel more empowered and in control. I then suggested she try a version of exposure therapy each time they came to class. From what I gathered, the child was scared of the water, and he felt that no one understood him and he was being forced to participate. The more he was pressured, the more scared and out of control he felt. Nothing was on his terms. I proceeded to suggest the mom ask him what he'd be comfortable doing. Then, each week, they could slowly build confidence and swimming skills on his terms while working toward the goal of fully participating in the class. In my head, I wanted to tell her that giving up completely and quitting class wasn't helpful, leaving out my advice on setting boundaries for his behaviors, especially when their emotions were controlling the situation. I didn't want her to force him to swim, either. I suggested giving him a sticker for each time he participated in class, even if it was only for a few minutes, building on this each week to earn something he wanted. Maybe he would start by sitting at the edge of the pool, then put his feet in the next week, then maybe stand inside the pool, and so on. She ended up thanking me and loving my ideas. I'm happy to report she took my advice and this story had a happy ending.

Setting expectations, limits, and boundaries with our children can be difficult, but it's necessary. Sometimes we need to be more collaborative with our children because their input is valid and valuable, but we can't give in to their every uncomfortable emotion. We can't let them off the hook when the going gets tough or it comes to trying new things, nor should we force them to do something. There is a fine line between the two. If they are physically, emotionally, and mentally distraught after giving it a good go, then you need to reevaluate. Have a discussion with them and try to find a solution. That's why I suggest going slowly, letting them have a voice, and making it play-based.

Chapter 17

The Power of Choices and Do-Overs

"Speak with your children as if they are the wisest, kindest, most beautiful humans on earth, for what they believe is what they will become."

— Brooke Hampton

THIS CHAPTER WILL PROVIDE EFFECTIVE, EVIDENCE-BASED methods on how to give children a choice to positively cooperate. This includes practical strategies on how to give children permission to try a behavior the right way and learn from their mistakes.

As we discussed in earlier chapters, when a child misbehaves it isn't necessarily because they are trying to be malicious. Many times, our sympathetic nervous system can automatically jump into gear when our child is acting out, and we fail to give them the benefit of the doubt. I've been there, too. It seems easier to jump right to a consequence when a child is displaying challenging behavior to diffuse it quickly, especially when we are in public. As moms, when our child misbehaves, we feel judgment from others, and we don't want to look like we are a "bad" mom or that we have a "bad" child. It takes a lot more time, practice, patience, and thoughtfulness to pause in these problematic moments and give our child a second chance to make a different, better choice. But once you learn these tried-and-true methods, they will become second nature.

The Power to Voice a Choice

Let's talk for a moment about choices. As an adult, we have a lot of choices to make on a daily basis, and sometimes it can be daunting and stressful. It might even feel like a chore. But for a child, who may feel defeated and powerless because they don't get to make many choices, a desire for empowerment may look like defiance or a power struggle.

There are many benefits when children are enabled to make choices. When a parent offers a choice to a child, the child knows their parent trusts them, and thus they feel empowered by the autonomy they are given. This autonomy fosters problem-solving skills, critical-thinking skills, confidence, responsibility, self-discovery, self-worth, and independence. Having the opportunity to make choices also helps a child learn about making mistakes and being more comfortable with failure. When a child has the power to make a choice, they feel like they have some sort of voice and a sense of control; therefore, they become more cooperative and won't feel the need for power struggles, tantrums, and other maladaptive ways to seek authority.

I know there are parents out there who are skeptical and resistant to giving their child choices. Some parents believe children should be told what to do simply because they are children. These parents believe they are in control just because they are the adult. I cognitively can comprehend the pushback, but I do not fully agree. When it comes to a child's health and safety, I am on board with a parent having complete control to guide their child to make good choices. Beyond that, it's more about the parent's insufficient need for power and control that gets in the way for them to allow their child to make choices. These might be the parents who didn't have much power and control as a child, so they continuously seek it in adulthood through relationships, including with their children. It is difficult for these parents to let go and allow their children to have any authority. These parents may believe that if they give their child a voice and allow them to have autonomy to make decisions, somehow their child is their equal, and they cannot allow that. I don't believe that a parent and a child are equal. And when a child makes a choice or has an opinion, that doesn't mean a parent has to give in to whatever the child wants. It just means that the child has a voice and is allowed to state their opinion on the matter so they have some sort of agency and can practice making decisions, which is a life skill they need as they grow into an adult. Restricting and rejecting a child's need to make a choice keeps them from feeling confident in their own critical thinking and stunts their growth toward autonomy.

A child who isn't allowed a voice or an opportunity to make a choice on any matter in their lives is the child who will be more defiant and power seeking. This makes the parent who is limiting their autonomy more upset when arguments, tantrums, and other challenging behaviors come to the surface, which then begins to sever the safety, security, connection, trust, and respect between parent and child.

Let's take a moment and talk about some play-based ways you can help your child make age-appropriate choices.

Choosing an Outfit

Each morning set out two or three different tops and two or three different bottoms for your child to wear to school. This gives them the autonomy to pick out what they want to wear from a small pool of clothing choices, as opposed to the overwhelming decision to make among all the clothes they own. Even though you are picking out a few parent-approved choices (with too much autonomy, they might fight you on wearing their pajamas to school), they have the option to choose an outfit that speaks to them the most that day. To make it more play-based and fun (which usually helps them choose more quickly), have them pick out a stuffed animal, doll, or action figure and have the toy point to the shirt and pants they want to wear that day. As they get older, they become more confident and opinionated about what they wear, so this will phase out around the middle of elementary school.

Choosing a Meal

Have your child pick out a family meal once a week. This not only helps them invest in the meal for that day, but it also enables their autonomy to make a choice for themselves and their family. With some guidelines (you can't just eat jellybeans and popcorn for dinner), give them a few preapproved menu options to choose from. If they can make dinner on their own, like cheese sandwiches and chips, for example, allow them to safely prepare as much of the food as they can with minimal interference. And if they want to cut the sandwiches into a dinosaur shape using a cookie cutter, let them make it play-based, too.

Choosing the Schedule

I have a feeling some parents reading this might think I'm a little outrageous. I assure you I am not. I'm just creative and think outside the box. Children spend so much of their day being told what to do, where to go, and how to act. What if they could live in a world where they were in charge for a day? Imagine how empowered they would feel. On a day they do not have any other commitments, such as sports activities, allow them to create their own schedule. Parents can learn a lot about their child by doing this. Start by asking your child what they would do in a single day and in what order if they had the power to do so. If they go to school, they can plan the afternoon, or you can wait to do this on a weekend or during a school break. This exercise gives the child the authority to take control of their day. Will they do homework or chores first? Will they eat dinner or take a bath first?

Feel free to give them some control on your busiest days. Even if you have to run a bunch of errands, this exercise is intended to help both of you. Let's say you have to go to the post office, the grocery store, and the gas station. You have to go to all of these places, but make it into a game and ask your child to choose what order you do them in. It shouldn't make a difference to you (unless your gas tank won't get you to the other two places first), so give them a little say in the matter. They will be so delighted you let them choose the order of the mundane errands that they should have better behavior during those errands, which will make your job as a parent much easier, maybe a little fun, and hopefully more peaceful.

The Power of Choices

Let's learn how to proactively and positively allow your child to choose to earn something like extra playtime instead of reactively taking something away. When a child misbehaves, adult caregivers often innately jump straight to a consequence. Often parents aren't willing to give a misbehaving child the choice to comply, as they feel they may not deserve the opportunity. However, after implementing this type of method in my home with my own children, as well as teaching and practicing it professionally for years with other families, I know it works and will make a parent's job easier. I know it takes more energy, time, and patience to pause and give a child the choice on whether to behave or misbehave, but it's worth it.

Let me share an illustration of a common interaction between a parent and a child.

Child starts misbehaving.
Parent: "I'm tired of you making a mess and throwing your

toys across the room. If you don't put your toys away now, you are going to go to your room and will lose your iPad for the rest of the day!"

Child cries and runs away or yells back or throws a toy at the parent, which angers the parent even more.

These moments can be extremely defeating and frustrating. And typically, a parent will start to feel remorse and guilt about twenty minutes later, once they are regulated again. Then the parent is in the position to make a repair with their child but remains frustrated and in the cycle because they don't know what else to do. But there is hope!

Let's try the same scenario this way:

Child starts misbehaving.

Parent: "I notice you keep throwing your toys across the room, which could break them or hurt someone. If you are able to calm your body and put your toys away right now instead of throwing them across the room, we can get a fun snack and you can earn ten minutes of playtime after dinner."

Child starts cleaning up.

Parent: "That's a great choice. I will help you."

This is obviously best-case scenario, and there may be more conversation on both sides before the outcome, but this is the general picture of what the positive choice cycle and earning something instead of having something taken away could look like. Just remember, boundaries over consequences and positive responses over negative reactions. For it to work effectively, parents need to remain calm and regulated. Parents also need to be proactive and teach their child what it looks like to pause and think and make a different choice instead of being emotionally offended and reactive. The more a parent tries this method, the more they will succeed in getting the behavior they want, and both parent and child will save themselves hours of distress and grow closer in connection.

The Choice Method

What happens if the child doesn't cooperate? What if they continue to make the same choice and become defiant?

Let's continue the conversation . . .

> **Child:** "I don't care about a snack."
> *Child continues playing or throws another toy across the room.*
> **Parent:** "Throwing toys across the room isn't safe. Something might break or someone might get hurt. I need you to put your toys away now, and I can help you. If you can do this, you can play before bed. If you can't do this, you'll have to go to bed earlier. Let's take a deep breath together, and then I'll give you a moment to make your choice."
> *Parents need to help their child regulate and then follow through with the predetermined incentive or consequence. Allow a moment to pass . . .*
> **Parent:** "What choice did you make?"
> **Child:** "I'll clean up."

Children will comply and make the best choice nine out of ten times. When they do, praise them so the positive choice is repeated in the future. If they continue to act out, there might be something deeper going on.

The Do-Over Method

When a child makes a mistake, instead of going directly for a consequence, give them the opportunity to try again and correct their behavior by showing you they know what they are supposed to do. The Do-Over Method is pretty straightforward but takes some practice. When a child breaks a rule, the parent simply asks the child to try again and show them how the behavior should have been done more positively.

For example, let's say a child is running down the stairs and the rule is to walk.

The parent says to the child, "Running down the stairs isn't safe. You can get hurt. Please go back up to the top of the stairs and show me how to walk down the stairs safely."

Or the child says something mean to their parent and sticks their tongue out at them. The parent says, "Those weren't kind words and actions. Let's try that again. Show me how to be respectful and say what you want in a kind tone and manner."

Then the child gets a "do-over" and doesn't get in trouble because they tried again and repeated the behavior in a more positive way. When you do this, you avoid punitive consequences by giving your child a second chance, which is a win-win for both parent and child. Remember to praise your child when they choose to comply and make the more positive choice.

If a parent wants to get extra fun and creative, they can make their child "do-over passes" that the child can use if they need tangible reminders. The child is allowed to use three to five passes a day from the do-over jar to learn how to control their body and their choices in a more visual way.

Chapter 18

Choose Your Own Outcome Adventure

"It is paradoxical that many educators and parents still differentiate between a time for learning and a time for play without seeing the vital connection between them."

—Leo Buscaglia

IN THIS CHAPTER, PARENTS WILL LEARN HOW TO PROVIDE age-appropriate behavioral boundaries, how to provide an incentive in lieu of taking something away, how and when to earn something back based on positive behavior, and how to provide your child with more authority by allowing them to choose a consequence after a problematic behavior. This shift in perceived control will allow children to feel more empowered, which will create fewer power struggles between parent and child and establish boundaries that determine outcomes for behavior. The twist is to make outcomes more of a choose-your-own-adventure strategy rather than to make them punitive. What is an outcome? It's a behavioral boundary with actionable steps.

When a child feels like they have some choice in what behavioral boundary they receive, a few things happen. The child may preventively not make a poor choice in the first place because they know the potential outcome in advance, or the power struggle and defiance are minimized because there is no anxiety around the unknown. When a child knows behavior expectations, limits and boundaries, and projected and possible outcomes, they can mindfully choose to misbehave or not because they know what's at stake. A parent isn't making emotional decisions or dishing out punitive consequences in the heat of the moment, and since everyone is on the same page in advance, it alleviates uncertainty and ambiguity. The important part is that children should be part of the process.

Choices before Consequences

As we discussed in the previous chapter, offering your child choices and do-overs when a challenging behavior arises may eliminate opportunities to give a behavioral boundary in the first place. Give your child the chance to behave appropriately and correct their behavior *before* a boundary is given. Don't just give a punitive consequence out of the blue or on a whim. Pulling the carpet out from under your child will typically only make your job more difficult and their behavior much worse. Plan in advance and make a list of appropriate boundaries that decide potential outcomes for minor and major misbehaviors. Make sure your child knows what these boundaries and outcomes are in advance.

When you observe your child doing something you do not want them to do, calmly and respectfully approach them and follow these steps as best as you can.

STEP 1	Reflect the behavior you observed: "I noticed you are jumping on the couch."
STEP 2	Teach your child why jumping on the couch is not an acceptable behavior: "Jumping on the couch is not safe and you could get hurt."

STEP 3	Remind your child of the rule about the behavior: "The rule is we sit on the couch. The couch is not for jumping."
STEP 4	Set a boundary and offer your child a choice to correct the behavior or receive an outcome: "You can either follow the rule and sit on the couch or you will have to get off the couch and come with me to help with laundry so I can keep you safe. I'll give you a minute to decide."
STEP 5	A child may respond immediately, and that is fine. If not, step aside for a moment and give your child time to process. Wait about a minute, then ask them what choice they are going to make.
STEP 6	If your child cooperates and sits on the couch, praise them for making a positive choice and following the rules. If your child does not cooperate and continues to defiantly jump on the couch, gently remind them of the outcome you discussed and follow through.

The Power of a Pre-Correction

A pre-correction is used to set your child up for success *before* they have the opportunity to get in trouble. Children will cooperate better when a parent is proactive instead of reactive. Follow these steps to ensure your child has the opportunity to behave and respond in a positive way, especially when you are going out in public. Before leaving the house, assess your child's emotionality. Expecting them to behave positively when they are hungry, tired, sick, or grouchy is a recipe for unsuccessful behavior for the both of you. Here is a recipe for success when you are going out in public.

STEP 1	Tell your child the exact plan so they can mentally and emotionally prepare. "We are going to the grocery store today. We are only getting what we need on our list, and then we are coming home." Share the list with them.
STEP 2	Let your child add one desired food item to the grocery list so they feel invested and empowered. Do they want a special snack that week? This will help them behave more positively while in the store. I suggest getting that item first or last on your trip. If you get it first, maybe they can snack on it at the store, or save it for last so they have a perceived incentive at the end of the trip.
STEP 3	Let your child know exactly what behaviors you expect of them at the store and give them support and encouragement. "I know you will be a good listener and use your quiet voice, use walking feet, and follow directions."

STEP 4	Teach and remind them what these behaviors look like *before* you leave. Define what the behaviors are that you want them to follow and practice (show them what a quiet voice and walking feet are, and have them practice). "A good listener is quiet and follows directions the first time I ask."
STEP 5	Inform your child of the potential outcome if they do not follow directions. "If I see you aren't following the rules, we won't be able to buy your special snack." Mind you, this isn't a threat; it is a boundary.
STEP 6	Follow through. If they follow the behavior expectations, praise them and tell them how proud you are of them. If they do not follow the rules, leave the store without their snack of choice.

Using these types of behavioral boundaries and positive supports while including the use of this specific language takes practice. As with anything, do the best you can. If you forget a step, give yourself grace and try again next time.

Determine Outcomes in Advance

The takeaway from this chapter should be to thoughtfully determine a list of potential behavioral outcomes in advance, rather than winging it. Keep your list easily accessible on your fridge or on an app on your phone so you don't give an impulsive, spur-of-the-moment consequence. This list will help you stay calmer and more prepared so you will not lead with your emotional state, which could be pretty dysregulated in the moment. Once you put a behavioral boundary out there in the open and your child hears it, it's hard to take it back. It's better to be consistent and follow through even if you regret the behavioral boundary in the heat of the moment. If you aren't consistent, you run the risk of your child not taking you seriously, losing respect for boundaries, and taking advantage of loopholes. Once your child discovers a loophole, you will be left feeling overwhelmed and frustrated, and it may even cause strife.

If you truly regret the behavioral boundary you give, you can turn to your child after a few minutes and tell them you were angry, you said something you shouldn't have, and you'd like to talk about alternatives. Normalize imperfection and mistake making, impulsive and dysregulated emotionality and decision-making, and the opportunity for everyone to have a second chance to correct their behavior. Make this a teaching moment. This may or may not mean they receive a behavioral boundary, but it gives you a do-over to come up with an alternative.

Determine Age-Appropriate Outcomes

How does a parent know what an age-appropriate outcome looks like? A parent's first instinct is to discipline their child in the same way they were disciplined as a child. Whether we liked the way our parents disciplined us, this is typically the first line of defense when we are upset. Unfortunately, it's punitive and impulsive consequences that are typically made irrationally in a dysregulated moment. That's why we want to be careful and calculated about what consequences we give our children in advance, so we don't panic and grasp at the first thing that comes to mind. Thoughtfully choosing an outcome takes time. And since children's brains are still developing and they have low attention spans (two to three minutes per year of their age), it's important to focus on their age and appropriate outcomes based on their cognitive and developmental level.

Children Age Three to Five (attention span ranges from six to ten minutes)

Children in this preschool-to-kindergarten age range shouldn't exceed an activity for longer than ten minutes, which in my opinion is still too long for a child that age. I personally believe from experience that a five- to seven-minute behavior outcome is sufficient for this age group. Many parents with children this age resort to a time-out, which is fine if you think your child needs to cool down and emotionally regulate, but I would try to change your language from punitively taking a time-out to positively taking a break. They will still be removed from the activity they are engaged in, but instead of being isolated in another room, which can feel like rejection, abandonment or shame, they can sit with you in a neutral area for a few moments (not with their face up against the wall in the corner or in their room). Removing them and pausing should be the only boundary they need.

Use a sand timer, a kitchen timer, or your smartphone to obtain an auditory and visual signal that they can watch and listen for when time is up. When time is up, offer them a hug, validate their emotions, and then discuss the behavior. Ask them if they know what went wrong and what they would do differently next time. Then move on. Don't keep score and hold this behavior over their head all day.

Children Age Six to Eight (attention span ranges from twelve to sixteen minutes)

In this early elementary age group, an appropriate outcome is about ten to fifteen minutes since it can take a child developmentally that long to regulate and reflect on the ramifications of their actions. In this age group, I recommend taking fifteen minutes off their designated technology time or going to bed fifteen minutes earlier. However, if the offense happens in the morning before school and your consequence isn't until bedtime, it's easily forgotten or not as effective because so much time goes by in between. I would recommend a more immediate outcome in this case. If you have the time in the moment and your child is regulated enough during this designated time span, they could draw a picture or write down a few words that describe their actions and what they would do differently in the future. This gets them thinking critically about the problem and identifying solutions for behavioral alternatives in the future. This is also a great age to teach children about natural consequences and responsibility for their actions. If they take a long time to brush their teeth and get dressed in the morning, being late to school is a natural consequence. If they throw their plate of food on the floor, the natural consequence is for them to clean it up before playing. If they defiantly refuse to clean their room when asked a gazillion times, a natural consequence might mean canceling a playdate.

Make Sure the Consequence Fits the Crime

When setting a behavioral boundary and choosing an outcome for a child's misbehavior, make sure it matches the severity of "the crime." Let's say your six-year-old threw their toy across the room and told you to shut up, so you respond by telling them they can't play video games for the week. That might sound a little harsh, yet so many parents resort to long-term punitive consequences for their children no matter what their child's age or their offense. If the behavior is more extreme—they hit someone in the face because they didn't get their way, for example—then I would understand setting a firm boundary and possibly taking a preferred activity away for the rest of the day. And in those more extreme cases, the child may need a higher level of behavioral intervention. Children under the age of ten have trouble telling time, so to them an hour can feel like a day or a week could feel like a month. I am exaggerating a little, but I want to drive the concept home. This is why a one-time minor-to-moderate offense should be treated differently than a repetitive pattern of severe misbehavior. The latter could mean something bigger is lurking underneath, and your child may need a higher level of care to address their behavior.

Time-In vs. Time-Out

In many cases, when our child misbehaves, we give them a punitive consequence and send them away for a time-out in their room or take something away that they enjoy, like a television show, a toy, or a tablet. But this isn't always the most effective parenting strategy to modify undesirable behavior. Instead of sending your child away when they misbehave and dishing out a punishment, ask them to join you to accomplish a task together like watering the plants, feeding the dog, or taking out the trash. Sometimes young children simply misguide their energy and it causes a problem, but all they need is an opportunity to channel their energetic behavior in a more positive way.

Young children typically do not have a multitude of chores, so make a list of age-appropriate tasks that would help you and the household. When they misdirect their behavior, allow them to pick one of the predetermined tasks on the list to do, with your help, instead of taking something away or sending them to their room. This way, you are still working on that connection piece and they won't harbor resentment or feel like you are rejecting or abandoning them. Instead, you are choosing to actively repair and rebuild a connection with your child.

On that note, avoid using a chore as a punishment. For example, let's say your child misbehaved, so you tell them they have to clean the toilet or go outside and pick up dog poop. When chores are punishments, especially the more labor-intensive, disgusting, or humiliating ones, your child will only feel shame and resentment toward you and will end up pushing back on all chores.

Ask Your Child What Outcomes Are Fair

I encourage you to have your child be part of the outcome-choosing process to help them be more accountable, understand "the why," and problem-solve collaboratively. Depending on the behavior they displayed and whether it's mild, moderate, or severe, you may have to give the outcome yourself. But if it's a mild offense, allow space for them to lend their voice and share their opinion. It doesn't mean that's the outcome you choose, but it will give you an idea of their rationale and what they think is fair. This collaborative communication will help you peek into the mind of your child and help foster your connection with them. They need and want to feel like you are in their corner, even if you are upset. They want to feel safe, and this is a way for you to convey to them that they are still loved even though they didn't make the best choice. Let them weigh in on a few options. My own children do this, and we usually end up negotiating and settling on something in between, which minimizes or eliminates the power struggle and makes them more willing to accept the outcome.

Punishment, Consequences, or Discipline, Oh My!

There is a difference between punishment, consequences, and discipline, yet many parents use these terms interchangeably. Knowing the difference between these three terms will help you determine what kind of parent you want to be. To me, the main differences between the three are the outcomes the parent wants to achieve for the child. And the language we use with our children matters.

In my perfect world, the word punishment would be eliminated from every parent's vocabulary. A punishment implies that the parent is in control and is trying to teach their child a harsh lesson because they deserve to feel emotional, verbal, mental, or physical pain as a result of their choices. In these cases, the child is paying for something they did, and the more it hurts, the better.

Consequences (or outcomes) commonly refer to a cause-and-effect relationship between something the child did and the effect of that behavior. For example, if the child is running in the house and bumps into a bunch of papers on the counter that fall on the floor, the natural consequence would be for that child to clean up the papers and put them back neatly where they belong. If a child throws their trash on the floor, the child's natural consequence would be to pick up the trash and put it where it belongs. If a child is pushing children on the playground, the natural consequence would be for that child to be removed from the playground for safety. This behavioral outcome is a teaching moment to reflect, regulate, reset, and reconnect.

A consequence should be given to provide healthy limits and enforce boundaries so your child learns right from wrong and builds skills to choose better behavior.

For a consequence to be effective, positive, and not punitive, a parent needs to first talk to their child about their behaviors and how these choices affected others. During this time, boundaries are reestablished and behavior expectations are reviewed. As the parent is teaching and connecting, an appropriate and thoughtful outcome for the child's actions can be determined.

Discipline is often used as an overarching term for how to teach children how to respect themselves and others and to learn right from wrong. Discipline teaches a child how to learn self-control. Discipline is the overarching expectations a parent has for their child and the way they run their home.

Now that you know the difference between the three terms, what fits best with your parenting style and the kind of parent you want to be?

Validate Before and After a Consequence: The Sandwich Method

When a child's misbehavior warrants a behavioral outcome, they need to know that they may have made a bad choice, but they aren't a bad child. Since children typically do not intentionally try to get in trouble, a mistake is often really just a mistake. They don't purposely try to do something wrong, and they often have immediate regrets. They also can't comprehend why they are getting into trouble in the first place. Remember, their impulsive and emotionally driven brains aren't even close to being fully developed. Children can take criticism to heart and internalize the response of their caregiver delicately, so before jumping to the punitive consequence, first validate their big feelings, then encourage them after the behavioral outcome is given. Think of it like a sandwich:

The bread: You are such a great child and I love you so much. You make so many great choices, and I am proud of how you can control your body and your behavior most of the time.

The cheese: Today, you lost control of your body and didn't make the best choice. Let's talk about a way to learn from your choice so it won't happen again.

The bread: I know it doesn't feel good to fix our mistakes. I believe you will work hard at trying to control your body in the future and make a better choice next time.

Not only does this sandwich method soften the blow, it helps you protect your relationship. It will help your child feel loved, secure, and safe as well as connected to you. And it will lead to better communication and cooperative behavior.

Giving Them Something vs. Taking Something Away

When I first presented this idea at a parenting workshop years ago, the room gasped. I remember it clearly, and honestly it took me by surprise, so much so that I had to pause my presentation. You would have thought I was feeding the audience liquid gold. They hadn't heard of this concept before and were amazed by the idea that this was even an option for parenting their children. It was a light bulb and aha moment for the parents in the room. Typically, a go-to consequence is to physically remove a child from where the offense took place or to take something away from them, and the more they love it the better. Some parents try to make it sting in hopes the child won't keep repeating that same problematic behavior. If it hurts, they will learn their lesson, right? Not necessarily. When you put it that way, parents sound like malicious monsters! A parent should try to avoid taking something away as a punishment, but instead set a boundary for safe and appropriate behavior.

Instead, flip the script. Instead of taking something away for bad behavior, have your child earn something for good behavior. That's right, you read that correctly: Turn the behavior into a positive they can work toward. This is a more supportive response that will foster a secure and safe connection between parent and child. But how does it work?

> **Parent:** I saw you pulling out pages of the book you were reading. Now you won't be able to read that book anymore.
>
> *At this point the child may now fully comprehend their actions and start crying from regret because their book is destroyed. Or they might keep pulling out pages defiantly.*
>
> **Parent:** I'll tell you what. Tearing pages out of a book isn't a good choice. Your book is broken now, and you won't be able to read it. If you want to earn a trip to the bookstore to buy a new book to replace this one, let's figure out a way for you to show me how respectful and responsible you are with your belongings. What do you think you can do first?
>
> **Child:** Silence. If the child is too young to come up with good idea on their own, you can offer a few choices.
>
> **Parent:** Let's start by picking up these pages and throwing them in the trash can. Then we can put away your toys. You can also show me how you can take care of your belongings and make good choices by making your bed, putting dishes in the sink, and keeping your room clean. Then we can replace this book and give you a second chance to show me you know how to behave respectfully and responsibly with your belongings.

Some parents may love this softened and unique approach, while others may loathe it and accuse me of unjustly trying to reward children for misbehaving. Won't my child walk all over me if I do this? No, they won't. If anything, they may respect you more. For those parents who still don't believe me, let me ask you this: Is punishing your child for making mistakes working for you? Do they really learn their lesson, or does your child eventually learn to resent you and defy you and continue to destroy things around the house because it gets them attention, even if it's negative attention? Do you feel close and positively connected to your child? Are they emotionally and mentally happy? Before you answer those questions, pause to reflect on whether you're truly solving the problem or just fueling the fire.

Earn It Back

If your child misbehaves or makes a poor choice but then quickly recovers and repairs, intermittently offer your child the chance to earn back what you took away. You may think your child will try to beat the system and start taking advantage of you, but typically the opposite happens. This isn't a loophole situation resulting from you not following through. This is a way to offer an olive branch and provide a second opportunity to do the right thing. Are you punished for every mistake you make as a parent, or do you offer yourself forgiveness and the opportunity to be a better parent the next time you interact with your child? Allow your children the same grace you give yourself.

Instead of enduring a punitive consequence that may make their behavior and your relationship worse, your child will bounce back quicker and try harder to behave more positively because they know they have a second chance to earn back what you took away. They also equate this with having a second chance at making you happy. Trust me, this grace will help your child's behavior shift quickly and also maintain the sacred connection you have with them.

Afterword

"Laughter is timeless, imagination has no age, dreams are forever."

—Walt Disney

There is no perfect recipe for being a perfect parent, and so much about effective parenting is about educating yourself, giving yourself grace, and learning through trial and error. However, focusing on connection and using play in your daily interactions with your children will bring significant positive change to your home, your parenting, and your child's behavior.

Acknowledgments

First and foremost, I want to thank every single person who has bought or believed in this book. I appreciate you and hope it changes your life as a parent and your relationship with your children.

To my husband, thank you for your support of my professional work so I could pursue this dream. I am extremely grateful of how highly you speak of me as a mother and for being on this incredible parenting journey with me. Our children are our biggest achievement together.

To my children, you are my most cherished playmates, my greatest joy, my proudest accomplishment, and the heartbeat of my world. You fill my soul with happiness and love, you are the center of my universe, and the purpose of my existence. You are my everything and I love you both with my entire heart.

To my parents, thank you for bringing me into this world and for encouraging me to always shine my light brightly, be the best that I can be, and never give up.

Thank you to all of my friends and colleagues who have rallied behind me and supported me throughout this book journey.

To Jill Marsal, my literary agent. You believed in me since the day I reached out to you in January 2022. You have been with me on this journey from the beginning and I am forever grateful to you for helping me every step of the way to reach my dream of being an author. If it weren't for you, I would not be here right now. Thank you from the bottom of my heart.

To Catherine Knepper, thank you for being such a big cheerleader to me and a pivotal part of my book proposal edits and writing process. Your encouragement and love for this book mean everything to me.

To James Jayo, thank you for believing in this project and giving me this book deal! You have no idea how grateful I am to you.

To Maya Goldfarb, for seeing this book through every single stage and all of the nitty-gritty details along the way, for being patient during my endless questions and requests (even my triple back-to-back emails in the middle of the night), for wholeheartedly supporting my creative ideas and ultimate vision for the book, for not giving up on me, and for always being so positive throughout this entire process. I am truly grateful for you!

To Ann Treistman, Devorah Backman, Kathryn Flynn, Gwen Davison, Lara Starr, Zach Polendo, Devon Zahn, Jessica Murphy, and everyone at Countryman Press and W. W. Norton, including but not limited to the editing team, design team, publicity team, production team, and marketing team, for all your support and for endless hours making this book come to life.

References

A4PT (Association for Play Therapy). "Play Therapy Makes a Difference." Accessed January 2026. www.a4pt.org/page/PTMakesADifference/Play-Therapy-Makes-a-Difference.htm.

Axline, V. (1969). *Play Therapy*. Ballantine Books.

Bandura, A. (1969). *Principles of Behavior Modification*. Holt, Rinehart & Winston.

———. (1977). *Social Learning Theory*. Prentice Hall.

———. (1997). *Self-Efficacy: The Exercise of Control*. W. H. Freeman.

Bandura, A., & Walters, R. H. (1963). *Social Learning and Personality Development*. Holt, Rinehart & Winston.

Berg, I. K., & Steiner, T. (2003). *Children's Solution Work*. W. W. Norton.

Berg, I. K., & Szabó, P. (2005). *Brief Coaching for Lasting Solutions*. W. W. Norton.

Bratton, S., Ray, D., & Rhine, T. (2005). "The efficacy of play therapy with children: A meta-analytic review of treatment outcomes." *Journal of Professional Psychology Research and Practice, 36* (4). 376–390.

Bratton, S. C., Ceballos, P. L., Sheely-Moore, A. I, Meany-Walen, K., Pronchenko, Y., & Jones, L. D. (2013). "Head Start early mental health intervention: Effects of child-centered play therapy on disruptive behaviors." *International Journal of Play Therapy, 22* (11), 28–42.

Caldwell, B. M. (1985). "Parent-Child Play: A Playful Evaluation." In C. C. Brown & A. W. Gottfried (Eds.), *Play Interactions: The Role of Toys and Parental Involvement in Children's Development*. (pp. 167–178). Johnson & Johnson.

De Jong, P., & Berg, I. K. (2002). *Interviewing for Solutions* (2nd ed.). Brooks/Cole.

De Shazer, S. (1985). *Keys to Solution in Brief Therapy*. W. W. Norton.

———. (1988). *Clues: Investigating Solutions in Brief Therapy*. W. W. Norton.

———. (1991). *Putting Difference to Work*. W. W. Norton.

De Shazer, S., Dolan, Y., Korman, H., Trepper, T., McCollum, E., & Berg, I. K. (2007). *More Than Miracles: The State of the Art of Solution-Focused Brief Therapy*. Routledge.

Franklin, C., Biever, J., Moore, K., Clemons, D., & Scamardo, M. (2001). "The effectiveness of solution-focused therapy with children in a school setting." *Research on Social Work Practice, 11* (4), 411–434.

Gehart, D. (2010). *Mastering Competencies in Family Therapy: A Practical Approach to Theories and Clinical Case Documentation.* Brooks/Cole.

Gil, E. (1991). *The Healing Power of Play: Working with Abused Children.* Guilford Press.

Gingerich, W. J., & Eisengart, S. (2000). "Solution-focused brief therapy: A review of the outcome research." *Family Process,* 39 (4), 477–498.

Ginsburg, K. R., the Committee on Communications, & the Committee on Psycho-social Aspects of Child and Family Health. (2007). "The importance of play in promoting healthy child development and maintaining strong parent-child bonds." *Pediatrics,* 119 (1), 182–191.

Gray, P. (2011). "The decline of play and the rise of psychopathology in childhood and adolescence." *American Journal of Play,* 3 (4), 443–463.

Gray, P., et al. (2023). "Decline in independent activity as a cause of decline in children's mental well-being: Summary of the evidence." *Journal of Pediatrics,* 260, 113352.

Grusec, J. E., & Goodnow, J. J. (1994). "Impact of parental discipline methods on the child's internalization of values: A reconceptualization of current points of view." *Developmental Psychology,* 30 (1), 4–19.

Haidt, J. (2024). *The Anxious Generation: How the Great Rewiring of Childhood Is Causing an Epidemic of Mental Illness.* Penguin Press.

Hayrynen, N. R. (2022). "Developing the wise mind: Exploring the experience of DBT." PhD diss., Michigan School of Psychology.

Iveson, C. (2002). "Solution-focused brief therapy." *Advances in Psychiatric Treatment,* 82 (2), 149–156.

Kiser, D., & Nunnally, E. (1990). "The relationship between treatment length and goal achievement in solution-focused therapy" [unpublished manuscript].

Kral, R. (1986). *Strategies that Work: Techniques for Solution in the Schools.* Brief Family Therapy Center, Wisconsin Institute on Family Studies.

———. (1995). *Solutions for Schools.* Brief Family Therapy Center Press.

Landreth, G. L. (2002). *Play Therapy: The Art of the Relationship* (2nd ed.). Brunner-Routledge.

Lee, M. Y., & Mjelde-Mossey, L. (2004). "Cultural dissonance among generations: A solution-focused approach with East Asian elders and their families." *Journal of Marital and Family Therapy,* 30 (4), 497–513.

Levy, J. (1978). *Play Behavior.* Wiley.

Linehan, M. M. (2014). *DBT Skills Training Manual* (2nd ed.). Guilford Press.

McKeel, A. J. (1996). "A selected review of research of solution-focused brief therapy." In S. D. Miller, M. A. Hubble, & B. L. Duncan (Eds.), *Handbook of Solution-Focused Brief Therapy* (pp. 65–98). Jossey-Bass.

Metcalf, L. (1997). *Parenting Toward Solutions: How Parents Can Use Skills They Already Have to Raise Responsible, Loving Kids.* Prentice Hall.

Mills, S. D., & Sprenkle, D. H. (1995). "Family therapy in the postmodern era." *Family Relations,* 44 (4), 368–376.

Nims, D. R. (2007). "Integrating play therapy techniques into solution-focused brief therapy." *International Journal of Play Therapy,* 16 (1), 54–68.

Piaget, J. (1962). *Play, Dreams, and Imitation in Childhood.* W. W. Norton.

———. (1962). "The stages of the intellectual development of the child." *Bulletin of the Menninger Clinic, 26*(3), 120–128.

Purvis, K. B., Cross, D. R., Dansereau, D. F., & Parris, S. R. (2013). "Trust-based relational intervention (TBRI): A systemic approach to complex developmental trauma." *Child & Youth Services,* 34 (4), 360–386.

Reddy, L. A., Files-Hall, T. M., & Schaefer, C. E. (2005). "Announcing empirically based play interventions for children." In L. A. Reddy, T. M. Files-Hall, & C. E. Schaefer (Eds.), *Empirically Based Play Interventions for Children* (pp. 3–10). American Psychological Association.

Reynolds, C., & Stanley, C. (2001). "Innovative applications of play therapy in school settings." In A. A. Drewes, L. J. Carey, & C. E. Schaefer (Eds.), *School-Based Play Therapy* (pp. 350–367). Wiley.

Rogers, C. S., & Sawyers, J. K. (1988). *Play in the Lives of Children.* National Association for the Education of Young Children.

Russ, S. W. (2004). *Play in Child Development and Psychotherapy: Toward Empirically Supported Practice.* Lawrence Erlbaum Associates.

Russ, S. W. & Kaugars, A. S. (2001). "Emotion in children's play and creative problem solving." *Creativity Research Journal,* 13 (2), 211–219.

Ryan, R. M., & Deci, E. L. (2020). "Intrinsic and extrinsic motivation from a self-determination theory perspective: Definitions, theory, practices, and future directions." *Contemporary Educational Psychology,* 61, 101860.

Skidmore, J. E. (1993). "A follow-up of therapists trained in the use of the solution-focused brief therapy model." PhD diss., University of South Dakota.

Sklare, G. (2005). *Brief Counseling That Works: A Solution-Focused Approach for School Counselors and Administrations* (2nd ed.). Corwin Press.

Sprague, J. & Golly, A. (2013). *Best Behavior: Building Positive Behavior Support in Schools* (2nd ed.). Cambium Learning Group and Sopris Learning.

Stalker, C. A., Levene, J. E., & Coady, N. F. (1999). "Solution-focused brief therapy— One model fits all?" *Families in Society: The Journal of Contemporary Human Services,* 80 (5), 468–477.

Taylor, E. R. (2009). "Sandtray and solution-focused therapy." *International Journal of Play Therapy*, 18 (1), 56–68.

Trepper, T. S., Dolan, Y., McCollum, E. E., & Nelson, T. (2006). "Steve de Shazer and the future of solution-focused therapy." *Journal of Marital and Family Therapy*, 32 (2), 133–139.

Vandenberg, B. (1985). "Beyond the ethology of play." In C. C. Brown & A. W. Gottfried (Eds.), *Play Interactions: The Role of Toys and Parental Involvement in Children's Development* (pp. 45–52). Johnson and Johnson.

Wang, M. T. & Kenny, S. (2013). "Longitudinal links between fathers' and mothers' harsh verbal discipline and adolescents' conduct problems and depressive symptoms." *Child Development*, 85 (3), 908–923.

Watzlawick, P., Weakland, J., & Fisch, R. (1974). *Change: Principles of Problem Formation and Problem Resolution*. W. W. Norton.

Willis, J., & Todorov, A. (2006). "First impressions: Making up your mind after a 100-Ms exposure to a face." *Psychological Science*, 17 (7), 592–598.

Index

About the Author

Dr. Kim Van Dusen has a doctorate in psychology and is a mom of two young children, a Licensed Marriage and Family Therapist, and a Registered Play Therapist. She has a decade of experience as a university professor, teaching master's- and doctoral-level students parent-child therapy and play therapy. Dr. Kim is also the CEO/owner/founder of The Parentologist, a family and lifestyle brand and blog about everything parenting with a therapeutic twist. Dr. Kim also has a master's in broadcast journalism. She can often be seen on local and national television and radio news programs and has contributed to dozens of publications like *Parents* magazine and Yahoo! and conferences like Mom 2.0 and Alt Summit. She has a social media following of more than 120,000 and is also the host of *The Parentologist Podcast*, which has been ranked as high as #104 in US parenting podcasts on Apple Podcasts. Dr. Kim has almost twenty years of experience working as a child therapist and also owns a play therapy–based private practice specializing in clients ages two to ten. She has a play-based, solution-focused approach to parenting that encourages fostering a positive relationship between parent and child.

You can connect with her on social media @theparentologist and www.theparentologist.com.